SO-AAI-806

ROOTS RUN DEEP
Our Ranching Tradition

Mackenzie Kimbro

© 2015 by Cola Blanca Productions.

ISBN 978-1-938850-17-2

No part of this book may be reproduced or utilized in any form or by any means, electronic or mechanical, including photocopying, recording, or by any information storage or retrieval systems, without permission in writing from the publisher.

Copies available from:

Mackenzie Kimbro
email: mkimbro95@yahoo.com
website: www.colablancaproductions.com

ECO Herpetological Wear & Publishing
P. O. Box 376
Rodeo, NM 88056 USA
telephone: 575-557-5757
fax: 575-557-7575
email: ecoorders@hotmail.com
website: http://www.reptileshirts.com

Printed in China.

HAPPY COOKING —
Kenzie
7/19/15

Malpai Ranch

Roots Run Deep
Our Ranching Tradition

Mackenzie Kimbro

Table of Contents

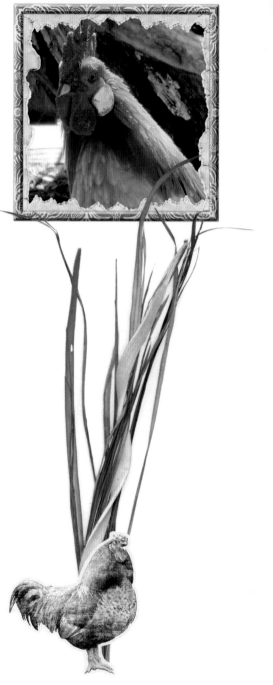

Chapter 3 - Traditions 42

Wendy Paul Glenn
November 22, 1940 - May 2, 2014
Her Legacy - My Inspiration

I know that usually book dedications are short and sweet and to the point. However, this dedication hits so close to home that I want to make sure it's adequate in reflecting upon Wendy and her legacy.

I called my grandma by her name, Wendy...not grandma or grandmother or any other expected name. We were a team, and I was privileged to be raised as her side-kick; and boy, let me tell ya, we had some great adventures!

Wendy meant so much to me that it was hard to figure out how to start this, so I decided to go with a quote. The late Maya Angelou once said, "I've learned that people will forget what you said, people will forget what you did, but people will never forget how you made them feel." Well, with all due respect to Ms. Angelou, I can safely say that no one will ever forget what Wendy said or did, and we most certainly will never forget how she made us feel. Wendy was the strongest person I know, both mentally and physically. She faced any challenge head on and head strong, knowing that she had all the support in the world and could overcome any obstacle that dared to get in her way.

Wendy was a passionate person, which showed in everything she did, whether it was archaeology, history, ranching, organizing an event or group of people, or being the one to keep us all in check.

Wendy didn't like attention to be directed toward herself, and was focused on working behind the scenes to make sure everyone else had what they needed to prosper.

She and I shared a very special bond, one that went beyond the stereotypical grandma/granddaughter relationship. Seeing as I grew up at the ranch most of the time, Wendy was more like a second mom. We spent more time together than most, and because of that she became my shoulder to cry on, one of my biggest cheerleaders, my rock. She was always there when I needed something, or when I had a question. If I fell, I knew better than to sit there and cry because Wendy would soon be by my side, telling me "Dog gone it sweetie pie! Now get up and dust yourself off, it'll be ok."

Wendy was raised at a place called Paul Spur, which was located west of Douglas, Arizona. Paul Spur included a limestone quarry and processing plant that was her family's business; and a village of employees, with their families, that worked in the quarry and plant. There was an elementary school, a grocery store and a Post Office.

Wendy's dad Alfred, they called him "Pos," had been attending Yale and his father had started the lime plant, but it was quickly going broke. Pos came home and went to the bankers and made a pledge that if they would give him 6 months, he would pull the business out of potential bankruptcy. He succeeded, and the operation flourished for many years. Pos eventually married Virginia Holland Paul and raised four girls at Paul Spur.

Wendy's dad and mom gave the girls a well-rounded life full of adventures and lessons. They traveled to Hawaii, La Jolla and Mexico and spent many hours in the ocean, swimming like fish and tanning like the natives. The girls learned to hunt and fish and ride like the wind. They were fluent in Spanish and that stayed with Wendy throughout her life.

Summertime found Wendy and her sisters boarding at the J Bar A Ranch with my grandpa Warner's family, the Glenn's. This evolved into Wendy and Warner eventually marrying and spending the rest of their lives as cattle ranchers in the deep southeast corner of Arizona.

Through the years, Wendy and Warner took on all ranching challenges. Wendy was a true pioneer woman, a cowgirl and ranch woman through and through. She had learned to cook and rather well. She could and would do anything inside or outside the house.

She could doctor and brand cattle, start pumps and grow a garden. Gophers were her arch nemesis and she was their worst nightmare. Warner and Wendy spent endless hours doctoring for screw worms, which was a daily chore.

For years they raised their own ranch horses, and Warner was always riding a colt. When it was time to start another one, he would have Wendy ride the one that was started and he would work on the next one. Unfortunately, most of them bucked, and sometimes long after Warner thought they were through that phase. Wendy rode a few and got bucked off a few; and when she did get bucked off, she always landed on her knees...not to be mistaken with landing on your feet!

In the middle of their young ranching life, Warner and my great-grandfather Marvin were also lion hunting all winter, sometimes away for ten days at a time, and if Wendy was not cooking in camp she was maintaining the ranch... Keeping in mind that their electricity was a diesel generator, there was no phone and no radio contact with my great-grandmother Margaret at the other ranch, and there was no TV.

Wendy calved out a lot of heifers by herself every spring, and through the years she and Warner performed C-sections on cattle, fixed prolapsed uteruses and grafted orphaned calves onto other mama's for adoption.

Wendy and Warner worked all the cattle together and Warner had a phrase that he repeated often, "Stand your ground!" It worked pretty well most of the time until one day they were trying to load a blind cow in the trailer. Wendy stood her ground as the cow came blazing around the corral fence and proceeded to run over Wendy. As she got up off the ground...not a happy camper...Warner exclaimed "Why didn't you move?!" and Wendy said, "You said to stand my ground!" and Warner said, "But Wendy... the cow is blind!"

Wendy and Warner always had 1 to 3 milk cows and so Wendy milked cows twice a day, made their own butter and ice cream; and of course they always raised milk pen calves and butchered them for beef. After the meat aged, they cut and packaged the meat in the kitchen.

The woman who had led a charmed youth, had become a true pioneer woman!

As with most ranch women, Wendy was an impromptu nurse at times, stitching up minor wounds on animals and people alike. One time Warner had cut his chin open and, not wanting to make the trip to town for stitches, sat down in the kitchen, where Wendy proceeded to start stitching. Luckily she started in the middle of the cut, and her not wanting to be wasteful, she put the needle through and then pulled the whole length of string through to the end! Warner admitted he may not be able to stand that method very long and called it quits on the stitching. Since the cut now had a stitch in the middle he took his chances on it healing on its own!

Because of the hunting, the summer ranch guests, and eventually the Malpai Borderlands Group, Wendy and Warner were always hosting guests and Wendy was the hub around which everyone whirled.

As the years went by, the ranching and hunting continued and our family became co-founders of the Malpai Borderlands Group. The office was in the Malpai Ranch house and Wendy was the Office Coordinator. The work load grew, projects expanded, and help was hired. The group became a huge success, representing politically correct, environmentally conscious ranching and preserving open spaces and wildlife corridors. Wendy was once again the "go-to gal," the hub.

It was stated that she had an amazing ability to defuse conflict and promote collaboration, and that she was one of the people that did the heavy lifting on conservation in the west.

In a days' time, Wendy could feed the hunting crew breakfast at 3:30 AM, make their lunches, help load the mules and hounds and send them on their way...then start a pump somewhere on the ranch...drive me 20 miles to school...come back to the ranch, put out minerals...pull a calf...feed the multitude of left over mules, horses, hounds and bulls...collaborate with someone in Washington, help Border Patrol with a flat tire, go back to town to pick me up at school, then back to the ranch to fix dinner.

Wendy poured her heart and soul into the Malpai Borderlands Group *and* our lives, and she and Warner were central to the welfare of the land and the future of responsible ranching.

Wendy flew under the radar, and she was "the power behind several thrones." She hated acknowledgement or credit for something, never wanted her picture taken and didn't really want to be interviewed for any articles. She was honestly humble.

Wendy nursed a lot of hounds back from injuries, milked out a lot of big bagged cows and had a knack for getting little baby calves to suck their mama's after some sort of hardship at birth. Believe it or not, Wendy never learned to rope! She was always the ground crew, flanking calves and working them on the ground. She could and would jerk down anything that the ropers roped.

My grandparents were a lifelong team, ranching in this rugged, dry land, feeding cattle through droughts, never backing down from anything. Wendy was a true 50% of the team. She was no frills and no "baloney."

Life was always an adventure with Wendy, and whether you knew it right away or not, you were in for the ride of a lifetime no matter what you were doing. Since Wendy drove me to and from school for the first 7 years of my schooling, then home schooled me at the ranch for two more years before I went back to public high school, we spent a lot of time learning together. Wendy was a huge history buff and absorbed every spec of information she could about our area. She took me with her when she went out and dug for Indian artifacts, and made sure there was a lesson in everything she said or did. Because of this, I learned to appreciate my surroundings, and value the history of our land, just like she did.

Wendy was passionate about archeology and searching for evidence and acknowledging the past. She wrote that she had spent some of the best hours of her life digging and enjoying the silence and excitement of finding little treasures. I tagged along on these searches for arrowheads and pottery, the whole time making my own collection of mostly rocks (they were pretty to me!) and Wendy just kept letting me collect them.

The museum at the ranch is a testimony of her passion for history and the pre-historic and historic native Indian cultures that inhabited our area. She cataloged every find, valued every indication and thirsted for knowledge of the Indians that were predecessors on this landscape.

Life with Wendy was always a field trip, whether I was in a back pack on her back or hanging on the corral fence watching Wendy work... We were a team.

Her favorite thing...searching for the past

Wendy would pack me on her hip, with my little fist clinging on to the back of her shirt with one hand and hanging out like a little steer wrestler as we blazed trails through the day. Wendy was a no-nonsense grandma... She and I had a few silent stand-offs and then we would both move on to more productive means of productivity! Wendy's vast knowledge of history, the land and nature made life interesting, to say the least. For two years after I had been trampled by a mule on the side of a mountain, she home-schooled me. When I returned to public schools, Wendy would supplement my education as much as she could including ordering the AIMS test study materials and walking me through the many lessons. Through the years, she helped me build an Egyptian pyramid and a medieval castle for school projects... Not life-size, but big enough to get in the way. Nevertheless, she kept them both...they are in the Malpai house on display.

Wendy planned to see me to graduation, but her life ended suddenly due to pancreatic cancer... Three weeks later I graduated as Salutatorian from Douglas High School, and I know that I could not have done that without her!

Wendy grew up a carefree young woman, with awesome opportunities of adventure, never knowing that she would one day be a force to be reckoned with...that she would leave a legacy so rich. She loved to hunt and was a crack shot with a rifle, pistol or a shotgun. She was a "cowboy," and she knew cattle and how to work them. She was no-nonsense, she treated everyone the same, she was dignified and honest and you knew exactly where you stood with her, and she did not beat around any bushes. She cut straight to the chase and she told you like it was. Many of us were admonished by her and yet she always gave credit when it was due.

Wendy was the true meaning of determination and strong willed, and she stood up for what was right. She never argued something that she hadn't already researched and knew the answer to...and most of the time in our everyday life...she was right! I've always looked up to her for her ability to make people set aside their differences and work for the greater good.

She was a good neighbor, she was a first responder to anyone that needed her, and she would get help in motion and rescue efforts accomplished. When Warner called her in 1992 with a severely broken leg and mostly detached foot, she took the truck and a twin bed mattress, splinted his leg, loaded him in the back of the truck on the mattress and drove him to the hospital... Warner was sure she hit every pothole in the process!

She was bi-partisan...as long as it stood for God and country, protecting our freedoms and protecting our land and our rights. She was Christian, morally sound and ethically strong. She always found the best in people. She was strong and true and she was not impressed by whom you were publicly or socially...but by whom you were within. She was fair.

Wendy acknowledged differences but searched out similarities so that everyone could get along and make progress. She made people collaborate, she got more done in a day than most did in a week, and she never once weakened. I'm proud of everything she stood so solidly for. Wendy was a pillar of good character, morals, ethics, and values. She was a beacon of light for anyone feeling lost or confused. She let you have your thoughts and beliefs... And yet in the end you somehow realized, and in some cases accepted, her take on the issue.

Wendy graced my life, enriched my life, nurtured me, commanded me the way only she could... Her no-nonsense character, dynamic and engaging ways have left a footprint on her family, friends, neighbors and the landscape that was so dear to her.

Anyone that knew her will be forever grateful for that, and those of us lucky enough to have been so close with her will miss her dearly.

Thank you Wendy, for everything. We will always love you.

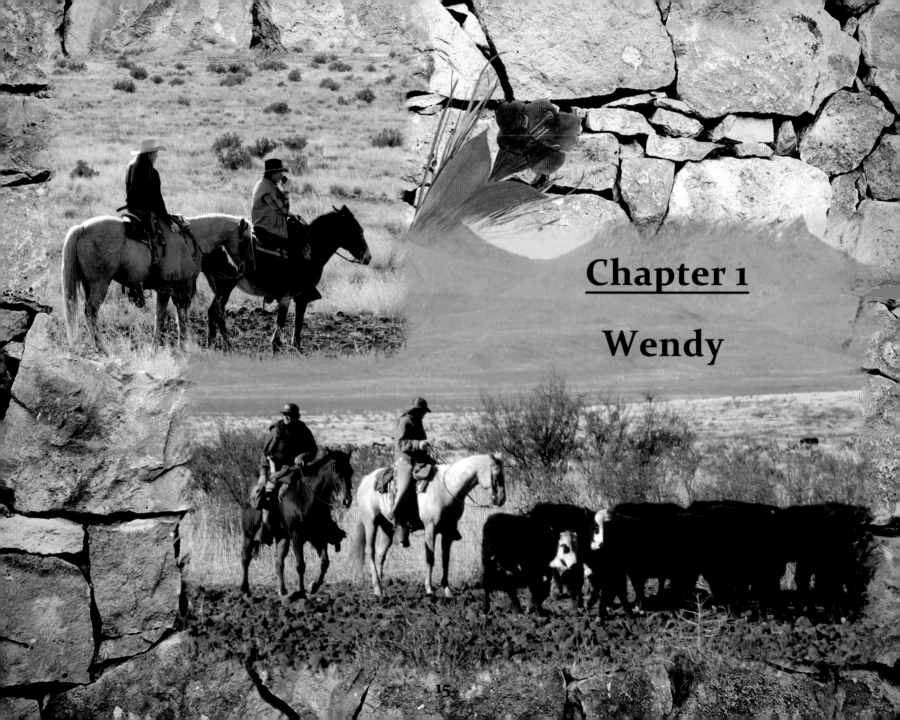

Chapter 1

Wendy

Wendy's Pumpkin Pie
Makes one 9-inch pie

1 c. sugar

1 - 14 oz. can sweetened condensed milk

1 c. pumpkin

2-3 tsp. pumpkin pie spice

½ tsp. salt

2-3 eggs

1 tbsp. melted butter

Mix all ingredients in a blender until creamy. Pour into an unbaked 9-inch pie crust. Bake for 15 minutes at 450°F, then 40 minutes at 325°F.

You might want to double the recipe and make several pies at once, they freeze well!!

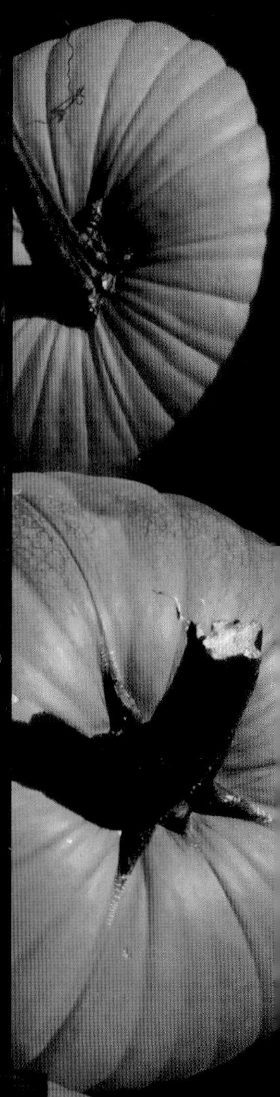

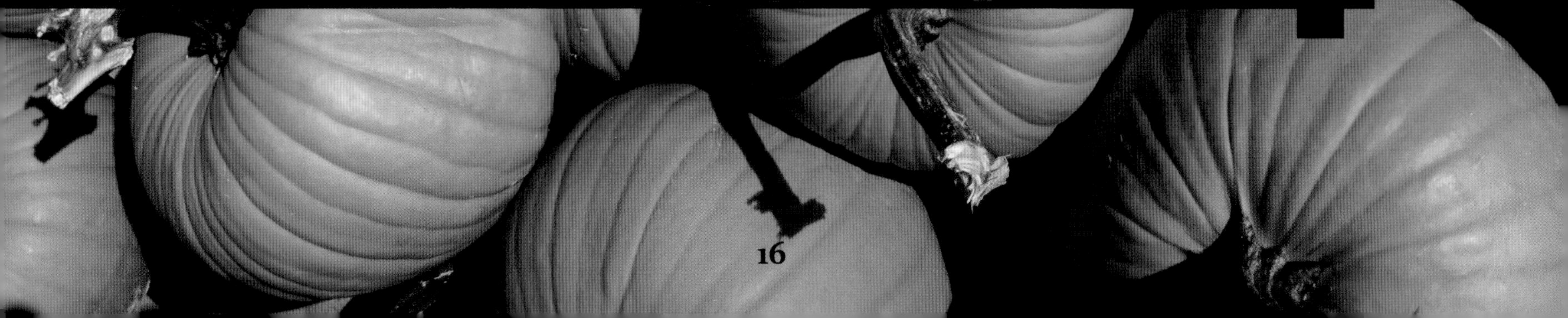

Pecan Pie

Wendy and "Crawler"

½ c. honey
½ c. brown sugar
¼ c. butter
3 eggs, beaten
1 c. pecans
One 9- inch unbaked pie shell

Preheat oven to 400°F.

Blend honey and sugar in a medium saucepan. Cook slowly over medium to medium-low heat, whisking constantly, until the mixture becomes a smooth syrup.

Whisk in the butter and beaten eggs until well blended, then add the pecans and stir to coat well. Pour into the pie shell.

Bake 8 to 10 minutes at 400°F, then at 350°F for 30 more minutes. A knife cut into the pie should come out clean when the pie is done.

Pear Pie

One unbaked 9-inch pie shell
4 medium-sized, ripe pears
Juice of ½ a lemon
¼ c. butter or margarine
1 c. sugar
¼ c. flour

3 eggs
1 tsp. vanilla extract
1/8 tsp. salt
1/8 tsp. mace
Whipped Cream

Peel, halve, and core pears. Brush with lemon juice and
place the pears cut side down in the pie shell with
the narrow ends toward the center.
Cream butter and sugar. Beat in flour, eggs, vanilla
and salt. Pour over pears. Sprinkle lightly with mace.

Bake for 45 minutes or until filling is set and lightly
browned. Remove from the oven and cool on a
wire rack for at least an hour before cutting.
To serve, top with whipped cream or ice cream.

You should serve the pie the same day you
make it. If the pears were pretty ripe,
the filling may darken the next day.
However, these pies do freeze well
when stored properly.

Marzipan
Makes about 1 lb.

8 oz. almond paste
2 c. powdered sugar
¼ c. corn syrup
3 drops any food coloring

Break the almond paste into small pieces over a medium bowl. Add 1 cup of the powdered sugar. Work it with your hands until incorporated (it will be crumbly). Add another ¾ cup powdered sugar, and work it in really well.

Pour in the corn syrup and work it until evenly blended. Spread the remaining powdered sugar onto a clean work surface, turn out the dough and knead until smooth and uniform, about 3 to 5 minutes. (If the dough seems too sticky, knead in more powdered sugar). Wrap the dough in plastic wrap and refrigerate for about an hour. After the hour, it should have the consistency of modeling dough.

You can eat the marzipan as is at this point... Or, here's how to make colored candies with the dough: Break off small pieces of marzipan, kneading in the color thoroughly until you attain the desired color. Blend the colored pieces into larger pieces of dough. Dust a work surface and rolling pin with powdered sugar. Roll out the dough to ¼-inch-thickness and cut into desired shapes using small cookie cutters to make candies.

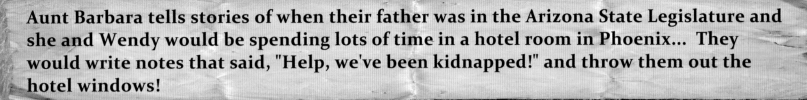

Aunt Barbara tells stories of when their father was in the Arizona State Legislature and she and Wendy would be spending lots of time in a hotel room in Phoenix... They would write notes that said, "Help, we've been kidnapped!" and throw them out the hotel windows!

They also had trained ponies that they would take into the house at Paul Spur when their parents were gone... I'm sure that went over well...

Who knew these two women would become true Women of the West.

My great-aunt Barbara Chrisman, a farmer, rancher, hunter and awesome woman. Wendy's little sister. One of my favorite people.

Wendy's Homemade BBQ Sauce
Makes about 2 c.

1 c. ketchup	¼ c. vinegar	1 tsp. chili powder
1 ¼ c. water	1 tsp. celery salt	¼ tsp. freshly ground black pepper
¼ c. brown sugar	2 tbsp. flour	2 tbsp. Worcestershire sauce

Combine all ingredients in a saucepan and cook over low heat for about 10 minutes, stirring occasionally. Serve over meat or rice.

Malpai Ranch

Wendy's Frothy Chocolate Ice Cream
Makes about 2 qt.

1 - 12 oz. can evaporated milk
½ c. whipping cream
¾ c. chocolate syrup
1 tsp. vanilla extract
1 tbsp. sugar

Put the evaporated milk into the freezer in a bowl until ice crystals appear. Pour into a mixer and whip at high speed until fluffy. Whip in whipping cream, then add the chocolate syrup, vanilla and sugar. Mix well. Freeze for 4 to 6 hours in a freezer safe bowl.

Wendy's Homemade Vanilla Ice Cream
Makes roughly 1 qt.

1 large pkg. instant vanilla pudding
¼ tsp. salt
4 to 6 eggs
1 c. sugar or honey
1 ½ tsp. vanilla
1 - 12 oz. can of milk or fresh cream

Mix salt, eggs, sugar, vanilla, and milk in the blender. Once the ingredients are well mixed, add the pudding mix and blend only until everything is combined.

Pour into a 2-qt. ice cream maker. Blend more milk in the blender to pick up ingredients that were left behind, then fill the ice cream maker until the contents are 6 inches from the top.

For a richer ice cream, use one cup of fresh cream plus one cup of sweetened condensed milk in the initial mixture.

Wendy's Cookies for Ice Cream Sandwiches
Makes about 16 cookies

2 ½ c. Bisquick	1 ½ c. crushed chocolate cookies	2 eggs
1 ¼ c. brown sugar	1/3 c. softened margarine	2 tbsp. white sugar
1 tsp. vanilla extract	2 tbsp. cocoa powder	

Combine all ingredients in a stand mixer and mix well. Spray cookie sheets with nonstick cooking spray, drop dough by the tablespoon-full onto the sheet, and bake cookies at 375°F for 15-20 minutes. The cookies will be firm enough to withstand moisture from ice cream.

Malpai Branding   Kelly and Jeff Rash, V.P. of Sales and Marketing, Priefert

Chapter 2

Trailing Warner

"Whose little baby is this?"

Warner tells the story of when he first met Wendy...

He was a four-year-old ranch kid at a Cowbelle get together at The Rancho Sacatal, in Dos Cabezas. As he and his mom, Margaret, made their way through the ranch house, her holding onto his little hand with a strong grip so he would not break anything, he spied a baby buggy. He grabbed the side with his other hand and as he peeked in, he saw a cute little baby girl.

"Whose little baby is this?" he asked and Margaret announced that it was Pos and Virginia's new baby girl, "Wendy."

Little did he know that for the most part, they would spend the next 74 years together, ranching, riding, working, living life and being partners in all that they would take on and all that the game of life would deal them.

Their engagement was glamorous.
Their wedding was the social event of the year.
Their honeymoon...
an adventure to say the least.

On the afternoon of May 14, 1960, Warner and Wendy drove the J Bar A red Jeep hunting pickup, loaded to the hilt with camping equipment and food, from Douglas to Antelope Wells, New Mexico. They crossed into Mexico there and proceeded south to the Sierra Madre mountains near Casas Grandes, Chihuahua, Mexico. Their destination was a large hunting cabin at the head of the Pierdas Verde River, owned by family friends and ranchers in the area.

For camp meat, Warner set out to bag a turkey, with his long-barreled .22 Colt Buntline pistol. He came back with a squirrel. Wendy, not having mastered the art of cooking yet, proceeded to cook the toughest sample of squirrel steaks imaginable.
Luckily there was a trout stream nearby....

Wendy's Chocolate Meringue Pie

Warner's favorite pie!

One 9-inch unbaked pie crust, or one 9-inch pie crust prepared using Wendy's recipe

4 squares German chocolate Baker's bar
1 ½ c. milk
½ c. sugar
3 tsp. flour
1 tbsp. cornstarch
¼ tsp. salt
3 egg yolks (reserve the whites for the meringue recipe)
1 tsp. butter
1 tbsp. vanilla extract
1 recipe Meringue

Bake the prepared pie crust, or use Wendy's pie crust recipe, until lightly golden brown. Set aside. Preheat the oven to 350°F. Melt the German chocolate in the milk over a double boiler. Remove from heat. Put the sugar, flour, cornstarch, salt, egg yolks and butter in a blender and mix until just combined. With the blender on, slowly pour in the chocolate mixture. Blend well. Pour the mixture back into the double boiler and cook until thick, whisking often. Once thickened, whisk in the vanilla and pour the mixture into the prepared pie shell. Top with the meringue, making sure to cover the crust edges. Bake at 350°F till the meringue is brown.

Wendy's Pie Crust

2 c. flour
1 tsp. salt
2/3 c. Crisco shortening, softened
¼ c. water

In a large bowl, combine the flour and salt. Using a whisk or fork, cut in the softened Crisco shortening. Add the water and, using your hands or a spatula, mix into a ball of dough. Roll out on a floured surface to make a 9" crust. Bake at 325°F for about 20 minutes until lightly golden.

Meringue

3 egg whites
Pinch of salt
1 tsp. vanilla extract
2 or 3 tbsp. sugar

Beat the egg whites until stiff peaks form. Add the salt, vanilla and sugar. Beat well and heap on pie, making sure you cover the crust edges.

Bake at 350°F until brown.

Alternative Pie Crust
Makes one 9" crust

1 ¼ c. flour
¼ c. sugar
½ c. butter, softened

This is a sweet crust

Preheat oven to 325°F.
Combine the flour and sugar in a large bowl. Cut in the butter until the mixture is crumbly. Mix with hands until a dough forms. Bake at 325°F for 25 minutes.

True Love

Macadamia Nut Buttermilk Pancakes
Makes 12 standard-sized pancakes

1 ¾ c. all-purpose flour
2 tbsp. sugar
2 tsp. baking powder
½ tsp. baking soda
¼ tsp. salt
1 egg, lightly beaten
1 ½ c. buttermilk
3 tbsp. cooking oil
1 c. finely chopped macadamia nuts

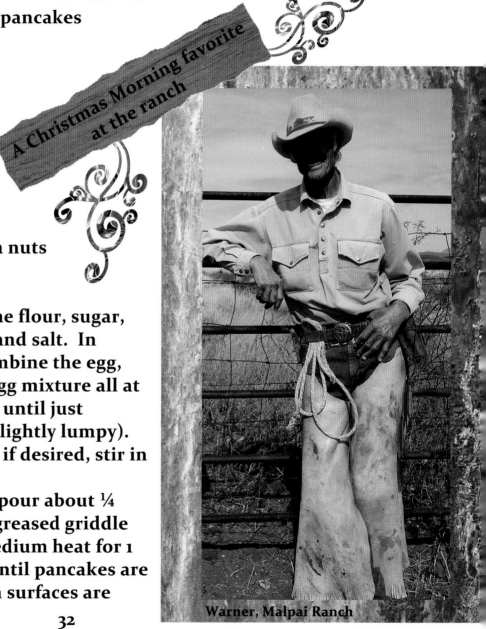

A Christmas Morning favorite at the ranch

In a large bowl stir together the flour, sugar, baking powder, baking soda, and salt. In another bowl use a fork to combine the egg, buttermilk and oil. Add the egg mixture all at once to the flour mixture. Stir until just moistened (batter should be slightly lumpy). Add the macadamia nuts, and if desired, stir in fruit at this point.

For standard-sized pancakes, pour about ¼ cup batter onto a hot, lightly greased griddle or heavy skillet. Cook over medium heat for 1 to 2 minutes on each side or until pancakes are golden brown; turn over when surfaces are bubbly.

Warner, Malpai Ranch

1938

Warner

If he had known what life would hold
roping bulls and bears and braving the cold

Chasing lions
running off mountains
riding good mountain mules
and raising and riding rock-footed horses

Pulling calves at midnight
pulling out bogged down
cows in "droughthed" out
tanks
fighting fire and praying for
rain

Picking guitar tunes and fiddlin too
dancing
and spending his life with the one woman that
he would love

Loving the land, his life, his work and his existence
He probably would not have changed a thing!
He is an awesome guy, a dynamite grandpa, father and
friend.
Warner, thanks for the ongoing legacy

2011

Our family has lion hunted through three generations, starting in 1947. The method used is dry ground hunting, trailing with "Walker" hounds, riding mules (the four legged kind), covering miles and miles of rough country, mostly in dry conditions and doing our best to manage the lion populations for the benefit of ranchers, and the local deer and Big Horn Sheep herds.

Marvin obtained his first hound in 1947, out of self defense! Lions were eating them out of house and home by killing calves and colts on the ranch. Soon, other ranchers were calling and the legacy began. Marvin and Warner followed in the footsteps of men like Ben Lilly and the Lee brothers. In those days, there was a bounty on lions, to eliminate livestock killers. Eventually, mountain lions would be added to the big game animal list and guided sport hunting became a business along with a more profitable method of continuing to manage the lion populations for the benefit of livestock producers. Margaret and Wendy were full time support for the hunters, doing all the ranch chores, cooking, pumping, feeding, moving trucks and trailers and rescuing lost hounds and sore, tired hunters.

In the late 70's, Mom became a part of the team, becoming a licensed guide and participating in the guiding, tracking, trailing and catching of lions.

Marvin passed away in 1991 and Mom and Warner continued the guiding business and the service of responding to lion depredation calls throughout southeast Arizona and southwest New Mexico.

Today, the business continues and with Wendy gone. I will try my best to fill her shoes at times, rescuing hounds and hunters, feeding, ranching, packing lunches and having a hot meal ready when the hunters return.

Jaguars

In 1996 and again in 2006, my grandpa Warner had the unique opportunity to photograph two different jaguars in southwest New Mexico.

Early one morning in March of 1996, Mom and Warner split up to cover more country and hopefully one of them would hit a good lion track.

Warner took the client and an assistant guide, named Aaron Prudler, up one canyon and Mom went up another.

Mom said it was a steep climb and she was cold, so she was walking and leading her mule up the trail when her hound "Maple" struck a fresh track.

All indications were that it was a lion track. Joining forces with Warner's team, Mom and Aaron brought the client at a safe pace while Warner went on with the hounds for several hours of fast trailing through rough country. Warner caught up with the hounds, and adjusting to the shock and surprise of baying a jaguar instead of a lion, managed to take 19 photos of a beautiful male jaguar. With a mind for unique situations, legalities and conservation, Warner let the jaguar walk away that day.

Ten years later, in February of 2006, once again while hunting lions they hit the track of what would be another large male jaguar, almost 40 miles east of the first in another mountain range. The spot patterns on the two jaguars were judged different, thus enforcing the fact that now two large male jaguars had ventured north into the United States from Mexico.

Lion Loin Medallions

You need one big Tom lion, one long day and night, one apple and one cement dam cattle watering hole, with water in it.

In 1956, Warner was 20 years old. He and Marvin were hunting in the Galiuro Mountains with a rancher named Alvin Browning and his Mexican cowboy. After leaving the ranch early that morning, Warner and Alvin went one direction and Marvin and the cowboy went another, both parties hoping to hit a track. Warner and Alvin hit the track of a big Tom lion. The country was rough and Warner went on foot with the hounds, letting Alvin take his horse to lead around the bad stuff. The hounds jumped the lion at sundown and bayed him on a bluff. Warner killed the

lion and gathered his hounds to spend a cold February night under an overhang in the bluffs. He was out of water, tired beyond reason, and hungry.

So, he built a fire, skinned the lion, fed the hounds lion meat and proceeded to bone out the lion's tenderloin. He cut it into paper thin wafer slices and placed them on a hot rock from the fire pit. Turning them with his knife and a stick, he cooked them until well done and that was his dinner. At dark, Alvin had taken Warner's horse and headed for the ranch, not knowing where Warner was and not being able to hear the hounds baying in the dusk.

During the night, Warner said that he would scrape the fire, coals and all, to another place in the cave, and then he would curl up on the hot ground with all the hounds burrowing and rooting in to snuggle with him for warmth. Early the next morning, he gathered the lion hide and skull and with his tired hounds, he started the long walk back to the ranch. He went to an old cement dam off in a deep canyon and drank the nasty water it held with gratefulness!

Climbing back out on a ridge he headed home. He heard a whoop from the ranch cowboy and went to meet him. He said the cowboy had a big red apple and that was the best apple he had ever eaten.

Not knowing where Warner had ended up the night before, Marvin had left the ranch at dawn that morning with a few hounds and they were trailing Warner, his hounds and the two night old lion track up from the day before.

In those days, 2-way radios, cell phones and tracking collars on the hounds were a thing of the unknown future.

Hollering back and forth to communicate and climbing a lot of mountains were the methods of the time and made for puttin' on a lot of miles.

Our Ranching Tradition

In 1896, the Glenn's traveled by wagon to the south end of the Chiricahua Mountains from Sweet Water, Texas. They stayed, homesteading in what is now called Half Moon Valley and Hunt Canyon. Our J Bar A Ranch was officially established in 1907 at the Hunt Canyon location.

Marvin and Warner were both raised and spent their lives on the ranch. Warner, Mom and I continue to ranch there. There are a lot of great stories of chasing cattle, good times, good meals, good friends, droughts, floods, Indian treasures found, lions caught and big bucks killed.

One story of how wild things got was when Marvin and his brother Bill were young men. They were trying to gather a wild cow and jumping her out of some brush, they both "built" to her with a competitive motivation. Bill threw a big head loop about the time Marvin moved in for the catch. Bill's loop scooped up both hind legs of Marvin's horse. Bill was tied hard and fast and of course, when the rope came tight, the wreck began... Marvin said he did not know what the heck had jerked his horse down and Bill was literally launched from his horse when it took the jerk. Both men and horses survived the incident and went on to catch the cow! That would be the true "Cowboy Way."

Another time, in recent years, when we had Brahma Bulls, Warner roped a big bull in a bunch of trees in a canyon. The bull brushed up and so the reasonable thing to do was for Mom to get off on foot and go into the thicket to let the bull chase her out... Warner promising he would not let the bull catch her! Mom said the bull had no chance of catching her... moments like that are when track stars are born!

39

J Bar A Ranch

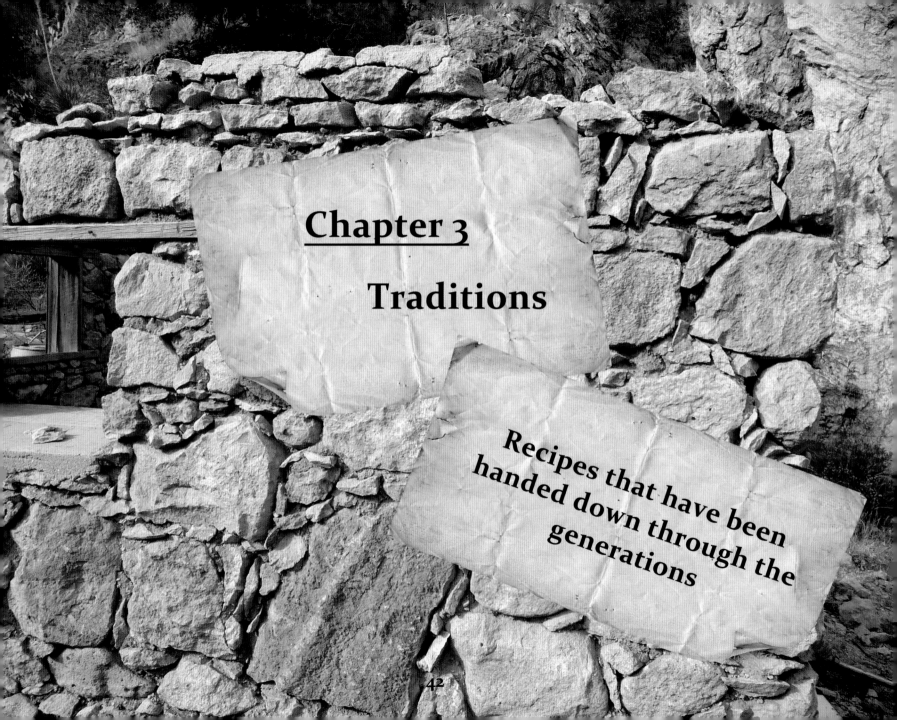

Chapter 3

Traditions

Recipes that have been handed down through the generations

Margaret's Meatloaf
Serves 12

5 lb. ground beef
3 pkg. Lipton onion soup mix
Salt and pepper to taste
2/3 of a 12-oz. can of evaporated milk
2 small 8-oz. cans tomato sauce
4 eggs
2/3 c. shredded wheat cereal, crushed
¼ c. onion, chopped (optional)
Grated bell pepper (optional)

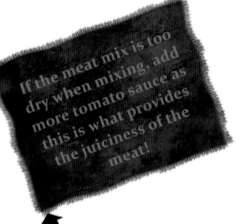

If the meat mix is too dry when mixing, add more tomato sauce as this is what provides the juiciness of the meat!

Combine all ingredients and put into a 9x13 baking dish lined with aluminum foil.
Cook at 375°F, 30-40 minutes, until almost done.

My great-grandparents, Margaret and Marvin Glenn, on the day that they got engaged. She was from a dairy farming family in Phoenix and he was born in Douglas at the Avenue Hotel and raised on the J Bar A Ranch. They spent their entire life on the ranch and our family continues the tradition there.

43

Meatloaf Sauce:

2 - 20 oz. cans pineapple chunks
½ c. light brown sugar
4 tbsp. cornstarch
¾ tsp. salt
2/3 c. cider vinegar
2 tbsp. soy sauce
1 large onion, thinly sliced
2 bell peppers, thinly sliced
1 - 4 oz. jar sliced pimentos

Drain the pineapple chunks. Save the syrup and add enough water to make 4 cups of liquid total. Set aside. In a saucepan combine brown sugar, cornstarch and salt. Add the liquid from the pineapple, cider vinegar and soy sauce. Cook and stir constantly until it thickens and boils. Once it comes to a boil, continue cooking until it's a thick syrup. Remove from heat and add the onion, bell peppers, pimentos and drained pineapple chunks.

Pour sauce over meatloaf and cook in oven another 15 to 20 minutes until the loaf is done and the sauce is bubbly on top.

Marvin was an avid guitar player and he even played the harmonica. He was self taught, learning many old cowboy songs and spending endless hours learning acoustic guitar and in later years, electric guitar. He could pick a mean "boogie-woogie!"

Margaret's Butterscotch Sauce
Makes 1 c.

¾ c. brown sugar
½ c. corn syrup
½ c. evaporated milk

Combine the brown sugar and corn syrup in a medium sauce pan. Cook and stir to bring to a full boil (this will take roughly 5 minutes). Remove from the heat and cool until a hand can be placed on the bottom of the pan. Stir in the canned milk. Serve over your favorite ice cream.

Margaret Glenn

Refrigerator Biscuits

5 c. flour   ½ c. sugar
1 tbsp. baking powder   1 tsp. salt
1 c. shortening   1 c. milk
1 c. buttermilk
2 packages yeast dissolved in ½ c. warm water

Combine all ingredients in large bowl and mix by hand.

Place in refrigerator and use as needed. Either hand form or roll out and cut rounds.

Place remaining dough back in refrigerator.

Bake at 350°F until done.

Marvin Glenn
1912 - 1991
Lifetime
Rancher and
Lion Hunter
J Bar A Ranch
SE Arizona

46

This recipe is from Maude Young, Margaret's mother. These tortes are one of Warner's favorite treats.

Maude's Date Nut Tortes
Makes about 12 tortes

1 c. dates, chopped
1 c. boiling water
1 tsp. baking soda
½ c. vegetable oil
½ c. margarine, softened
1 c. sugar
2 eggs
1 tsp. vanilla
1 ¾ c. sifted flour
1 tsp. baking powder
1 c. semi-sweet chocolate chips
1 c. chopped pecans

Preheat oven to 350°F.
Mix the dates, boiling water and baking soda. Set aside to cool.
Combine the vegetable oil, margarine, sugar, eggs, vanilla, flour and baking powder until well mixed. Stir in the cooled date mixture. Add the chocolate chips and pecans. Spoon into a lightly greased cupcake tin and bake at 350°F for 18 to 25 minutes.

Margaret's Ice Box Cookies
Makes about 24 cookies

1 lb. butter
2 c. sugar
2 eggs, beaten
4 c. flour

Mix all ingredients together in a
stand mixer. Lay out a big piece
of plastic wrap, place dough onto
lower third of wrap, use your
hands to form a log, and then
roll and wrap the log in the
plastic. Refrigerate or freeze,
slice and bake on a lightly
greased cookie sheet at
325°F until golden brown.

Margaret's Hot Chocolate Mix
Makes a winter's supply of hot cocoa!

10 qt. powdered milk
2 - 1 lb. boxes Nestle Quick powdered instant chocolate milk
½ c. powdered sugar
1 large 35.3-oz. jar non-dairy creamer
Sugar, to taste, if desired

Mix well and store in an airtight container.

To serve, fill cup 1/3 full with mix.

Add boiling water.

Stir and serve.

J Bar A, 1950s

Margaret's Rolls
Makes 24 rolls

Dissolve 2 packages of yeast in ½ c. warm water.

Scald 1 ½ c. milk. Add 2 tsp. sugar and 2 tsp. shortening.

Add sugar mix to yeast with 2 c. flour and 1 tsp. salt. Mix well and add 1 beaten egg and 2 more c. of flour.

Let rise in a large bowl, covered with a thin towel, until almost double. Roll out, cut into rounds, dip in melted butter and fold over.

Let rise again until almost double and bake at 450°F till lightly golden.

Hunt Canyon, J Bar A Ranch

Fudge and Floods

The J Bar A is a place filled with memories and great stories. Marvin and Margaret lived their lives ranching and guiding lion hunts there. They supplemented their income by hosting kids and teens in the summer as a guest ranch.

It was an awesome experience for the city youth that came and went. They learned to work cattle, ride, garden, be a family unit, honor the Lord, dance, play "cowboy poker" and be a part of a team. They learned to pray for rain, appreciate the simple life of growing your own food, helping to clear the table after a meal, doing dishes, making your bed, cleaning corrals and any other general ranch duty.

A simple, yummy tradition that Margaret carried out every time the creek flooded was to make a fresh batch of fudge! Most chefs won't make a batch of fudge when the humidity is high...yet Margaret made dozens of batches over the years and it never failed.

Margaret's Fudge
Makes 3 lbs.

Combine 3 c. sugar, 3/4 c. margarine and 2/3 c. milk in a heavy 2-1/2 qt. saucepan; bring to a full rolling boil, stirring constantly. Continue boiling for 5 minutes over medium heat or until a candy thermometer reaches 234°F, stirring constantly to prevent scorching. Remove from heat and stir in 1 -12 oz. bag of semi-sweet chocolate chips until melted.

Add 1 - 7 oz. jar of marshmallow crème, 1 c. chopped pecans and 1 tsp. vanilla; beat until well blended. Pour into a greased 9x13 pan. Cool at room temperature, then cut into squares.

The venison used in this recipe has always been Arizona Coues Deer. The field dressing and initial care of the deer from field to freezer makes a huge difference in the flavor of the meat.

Getting the deer gutted, skinned and the meat cooled out is high priority.

Our family has always had a walk-in cold box on the ranches and so we are able to age our venison. That too helps the flavor.

Easy Venison Loin Steaks

Venison Loin
Unseasoned meat tenderizer
Melted butter
A campfire

Trim out loin from all bone and fat.

Slice the meat about ½ inch thick. Sprinkle with unseasoned tenderizer.

Let sit for at least half an hour. Dip the steaks in melted butter and put on the grill over campfire coals.

The butter will catch fire on the meat and sear it. Turn the meat over, sear the second side, and eat immediately.

Be careful not to overcook it!

53

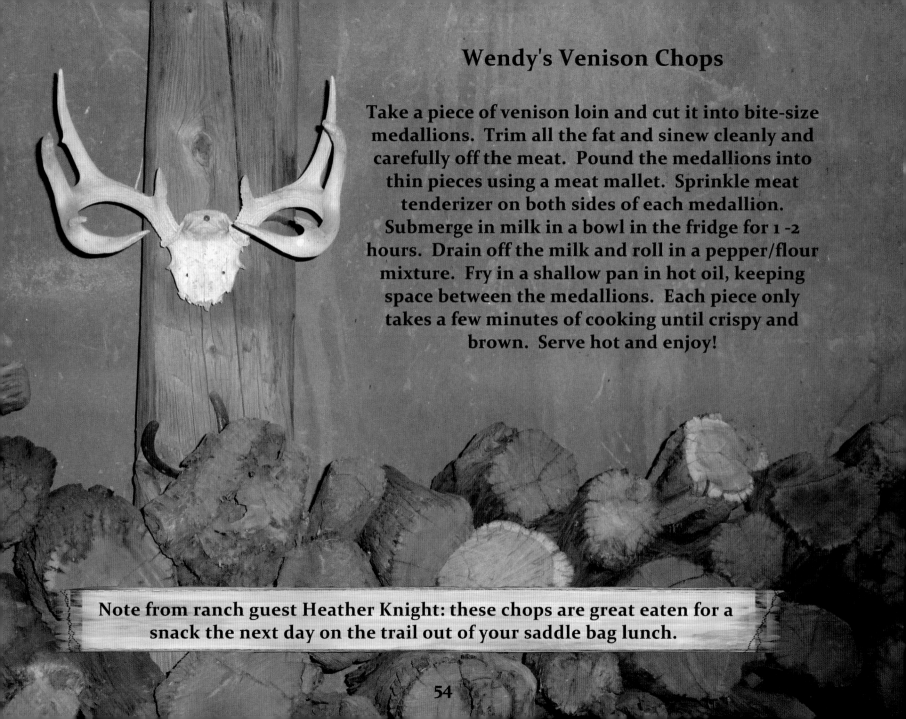

Wendy's Venison Chops

Take a piece of venison loin and cut it into bite-size medallions. Trim all the fat and sinew cleanly and carefully off the meat. Pound the medallions into thin pieces using a meat mallet. Sprinkle meat tenderizer on both sides of each medallion. Submerge in milk in a bowl in the fridge for 1-2 hours. Drain off the milk and roll in a pepper/flour mixture. Fry in a shallow pan in hot oil, keeping space between the medallions. Each piece only takes a few minutes of cooking until crispy and brown. Serve hot and enjoy!

Note from ranch guest Heather Knight: these chops are great eaten for a snack the next day on the trail out of your saddle bag lunch.

Hot Buttered Rum Sauce
Makes 2 c.

½ c. packed brown sugar
½ c. butter
2/3 c. heavy whipping cream
¼ c. rum (or rum extract, if
preferred)

Mix all ingredients in 1 ½-quart
saucepan.
Heat to boiling over medium
heat, stirring constantly.
Boil 3 to 4 minutes, continuing
to stir constantly, until slightly
thickened.
Serve warm over fresh fruit,
cake, or ice cream!

Store covered in refrigerator.

Wendy Paul
Douglas High School

Sunset, Malpai Ranch

Caramel Corn
Makes 3 qt. popcorn

1 c. brown sugar
¾ c. water
3 tbsp. light corn syrup
1 c. white sugar
3 tbsp. margarine
3 qt. popcorn, popped

Mix brown sugar, water, corn syrup, sugar and margarine in a large kettle. Cook to hard-ball stage on a candy thermometer (250°F). Pour popcorn into syrup and stir, over medium heat, until all popcorn is coated and dry.

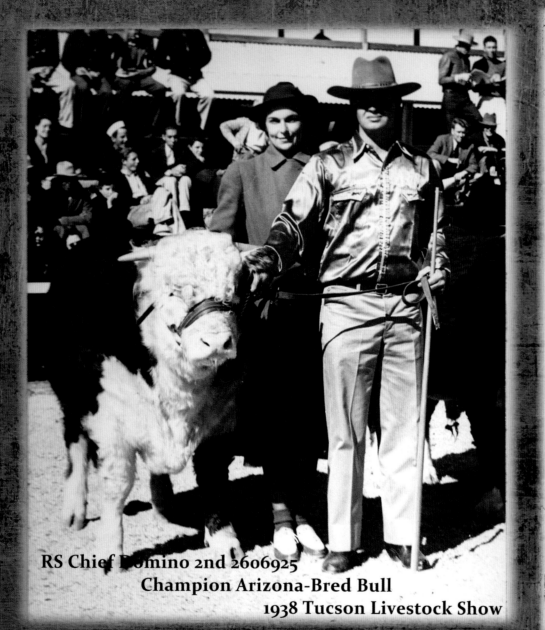

RS Chief Domino 2nd 2606925
Champion Arizona-Bred Bull
1938 Tucson Livestock Show

My great-grandparents, Alfred and Virginia Paul, with a Champion Bull raised by my great-great-grandparents Walter and Alice Holland on the Rancho Sacatel.

Who knew that 76 years later I would be showing market steers as part of my FFA Supervised Agricultural Experience!

Times and cattle have changed!

These recipes are word for word by their makers. In 1935, life was simple, and recipes were too! It was expected that everyone knew how to make something like "sweetened whipped cream" ...

"Party Dessert"
Recipe from the kitchen of Daisy, the original Rancho Sacatal Cook!

Combine quartered marshmallows, pineapple cut into pieces, and chopped maraschino cherries. Chill for several hours in the fridge.

Just before serving, fold in sweetened whipped cream and garnish with a cherry atop each serving.

Tutu's Coconut Macaroons
Makes about 3 dozen

2/3 c. unbleachesd all-purpose flour
5 c. shredded coconut
¼ tsp. salt
1 - 14 oz. can sweetened condensed milk
2 tbsp. vanilla extract

Preheat oven to 350°F. Grease a baking sheet.
Mix flour, coconut and salt; add sweetened condensed milk and vanilla. Stir well to make a thick batter.
Drop batter by ¼-cup-fulls onto the greased baking sheet.
Bake about 18 minutes, or until golden brown. Remove at once, cool.

Tutu's "Vege" Salad Bowl

A good way to utilize left-over Romaine leaves. First sharpen chef's knife.
Trim the Romaine, just leaving the best crisp, white part and a small amount of green. Wash and dry thoroughly, then cut up in rather small pieces. Dump into bottom of bowl.
Slice hard-cooked eggs and cut into pieces. Add to lettuce.
Take some boiled red new potatoes, slice about ½ to ¾-inch thick, then into cubes. Add.
Now cut the end off a nice, pliable, room-temperature lemon. Cover end with cloth and squeeze generously over potatoes.
Sprinkle generously with salt.
Wipe clean, remove stems and slice into medium thickness slices some nice, fresh mushrooms. Add to bowl.
Drip some marinade, either use your own recipe or the marinade out of a pickled mushroom or artichoke jar, all over the mushrooms. Shake on some more salt.
Pick fresh parsley, wash and dry and cut coarsely. Cover mushrooms with this.
Add several spoonfuls of capers. Taste and add more salt if necessary. Toss thoroughly and serve with a soup spoon. Serve at room temperature.

Suggestion: It may be tastier if you let it sit in the bowl and "season" for a few minutes-not in the fridge. Serve in large bowls. Serve with buttered homemade bread toast and hot bouillon in big mugs.

Alfred and Virginia Paul, "Pos" and "Tutu."
Avid deep-sea fishing partners, they caught a lot of Marlin through the years. One specific trophy Marlin that they landed ended up mounted and hanging behind the registration desk of the Playa De Cortez Hotel in Cabo San Lucas, Baja.

My grandma Wendy told stories of her childhood, spending time on the beaches of Guaymas, Mexico with her parents. They would camp on the sand and watch for the fishing boats to return to the villages in the evening. "Pos" would wave a bottle of whiskey and a fisherman in a little rowboat would leave the fishing vessels and bring a huge basket of the catch of the day to trade for the whiskey.

Christmas Tree Hunting

Among our many adventures, Wendy and I were always elected to go cut a Christmas tree for the ranch. Usually, Mom and Warner were guiding hunters, leaving Wendy and I as the committee in charge of rounding up the perfect tree, getting it back to the ranch, and getting it into the house...which was usually the most difficult part! Surprising how small the front door is...

Mom would buy us a tree permit. We would make the trip to the mountains with our hand saws in hand and Wendy's white Chevy truck.
Most years worked out well... But one year, we negated to read the permit and see that we were supposed to cut a tree over 100 feet from the road, less than 6 inches across at the base and not a split/double trunk...Yep, we failed to master any of the three.
It is amazing how much a tree grows after it's lying on the ground and the trunk has split apart after cutting. We always thought we were ready to load, but this notion was inevitably tested about halfway through, when we realized the bed of the truck was completely full of tree. The real challenge presented itself when we struggled to get the whole tree through the front door of the house. But always in simple Wendy fashion, we got er' done.

Another year, as we were attempting to make sure we were over 100 feet from the main road, we drove off on a little ranch road to a stock tank. In doing so we had to cross a small canyon and with some misjudgment, we got stuck. Wendy promptly put the truck in reverse and revved it up, firing backward up a little hill and straight into a tree... Tore the side mirror off the door and put a large dent in the bumper. On the way home, Wendy said, "Don't tell Warner or your mother." Hmmm, well... when Mom saw the dent and the missing mirror, she asked what we had been up to. I stood strong and said, "Ask Wendy..."

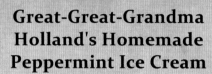

**Great-Great-Grandma
Holland's Homemade
Peppermint Ice Cream**

2 ¼ large peppermint sticks
(or a generous ½ lb.)
2 c. heavy cream
1 pint milk

Break the peppermint sticks
into very small pieces. Pour
one cup of heavy cream over
them and let set overnight in
the refrigerator. In the
morning, add another cup of
heavy cream, along with the
milk. Pour into the bowl of
an ice cream maker and
freeze. Use an old-fashioned
ice cream maker that uses
rock salt.

Circa 1935!

64

Chapter 4

Cola Blanca Productions

My registered livestock brand is a Coues Deer head, which is called Cola Blanca in Spanish. I am calling my business Cola Blanca Productions.
The influences in my life have been heavy and well taken. I appreciate my heritage, my family, my friends and the opportunities that have come my way.

This chapter contains recipes that I have developed. It is my hope to continue cooking, ranching and hunting.

The first lion I killed! A calf killer...

Tequila Onions

2 medium to large white onions
2 sticks (1 c.) butter
1 c. tequila
2 tsp. Montreal steak seasoning
OR Salt and Pepper

Peel the onions and slice them into rings. Set them aside.

In a large skillet, melt the butter completely over medium-high heat. Reduce the heat to medium-low and slowly add the tequila. Stir the liquid, then add in the onions and toss to coat. Cover the skillet and simmer until the onions are translucent, tossing the onions around in the cooking liquid occasionally during the cooking process. When the onions are close to done, season them with either salt and pepper or the Montreal steak seasoning.

If you are planning to use these onions on top of burgers, this recipe will make enough for about 10 burgers.

You can also find this recipe in the Hearty Beef and Tortilla Strip Soup! The aroma that wafts throughout your kitchen while these onions cook is to die for! YUM!!!

Burger Bar

Now and then you get *very* short notice and need to cook a big meal for a hungry crowd! Burgers are always a good option and a "Burger Bar" elevates the norm. Here are some of our favorite components.

1 Take your favorite patty recipe and boost it's flavor by adding:
Chopped Vidalia Onions
Minced Garlic
Oregano or Thyme
Cheese

2 Besides the classic toppings and condiments, here's a round up of fresh ideas for wild & tasty burger embellishments:
Green Chile Strips
Bacon
Avocado Slices
Guacamole
Sliced Fresh Jalapenos
Pickled Jalapeno Slices
Salsa
Tequila Onions
Tomato Chutney

Warm Tomato Chutney

1 - 4 oz. can chopped green chili, drained
1 - 14.5 oz. can Italian seasoned diced tomatoes
1/4 c. beef broth

Combine in saucepan and bring to boil.
Drain and serve hot.

Chunky Corn Salsa
Makes about 6 c.

2 Roma tomatoes, diced
¼ white onion, finely chopped
½ green bell pepper, chopped
1 tsp. minced garlic
1 - 15.25 oz. can corn
1 - 4 oz. can green chile
1 tsp. garlic powder
5 tbsp. lime juice
1 tbsp. cilantro, finely chopped
Salt and pepper to taste

Combine all ingredients in a large glass bowl and toss to combine. Let sit, covered, in the refrigerator for 6-8 hours or overnight to let the veggies marinate and become super flavorful.

Montreal Roasted Veggies
Serves 4-6

2 medium-sized zucchini, cut into thin strips or small chunks
2 medium-sized yellow squash, cut into thin strips or small chunks
1 stick (1/2 c.) butter, melted
1 small 14.5-oz. can low-sodium chicken broth
Montreal steak seasoning

Preheat oven to 350°F.
In a roaster pan or 9x13 casserole dish, pour in the squash and zucchini and toss to combine. In a bowl, combine the melted butter, chicken broth and seasoning. Pour the seasoned butter mixture over the vegetables and toss to coat. Put in the oven and cook at 350°F for 20-30 minutes until fork tender.

Twist: You can also use beef broth if you're serving these veggies with a beef dish, or if you just want them to have a heartier flavor!

Spicy Hominy Tomato Fiesta
Serves 10-12

1 gallon can white hominy, drained and
rinsed
1 - 10 oz. can Rotel
2 - 20 oz. cans corn, drained and rinsed
3 tbsp. butter

Combine the hominy, Rotel, corn, and
butter in a shallow stove-top pot. Heat
over medium heat until hot and ready to
serve.

TWIST:
For a milder version, substitute 1 - 14.5 oz.
can of Italian seasoned diced tomatoes
and 1 - 4 oz. can of mild green chiles for
the Rotel.

Kitchen Sink Hominy Blend
(Family-size!)

4 medium to large potatoes
1 - 20 oz. can hominy
1 - 20 oz. can kernel corn
1 - 1 qt. can ranch-style beans
1-2 small cans Italian Seasoned diced tomatoes (or regular diced tomatoes, but you'll need to add basil, oregano, and garlic seasoning to them to taste)
1 - 20 oz. can beef broth
¼ purple onion, diced
Lemon Pepper and Salt, to taste
Grated cheese and tortilla strips, to garnish

Sauté diced onion with lemon pepper and salt. Set aside. Peel, dice and pan fry the potatoes in the skillet where the onions were cooked, trying to stop frying them just before they turn mushy. Set aside.
Combine the hominy, corn, beans, tomatoes, beef broth and onions in a large casserole dish. Add the potatoes (or cooked rice, if preferred).
Heat and bring to a bubbly mixture in the oven or on the stovetop. Once bubbling, top with a thick layer of grated cheese and tortilla strips.
Cover and let the cheese melt. Serve immediately.

*For a slightly spicier variation, you can substitute Rotel tomatoes with chile instead of the Italian seasoned diced tomatoes.

A client's lion

Lion hounds to be....

Italian Eggplant Pasta

Serves 6-8

1 lb. pasta shells

½ white eggplant

3 eggs, beaten

Rice Flour and Italian breadcrumbs, amount varies depending on thickness desired for coating

½ red bell pepper, chopped

2 tomatoes, chopped

Shredded Parmesan cheese

1 - 16 oz. can garbanzo beans

1 - 15.25 oz. can corn

1 -4 oz. can diced green chile

½ yellow bell pepper, chopped

Shredded Mozzarella cheese

Boil pasta as directed on the package. Drain, lightly drizzle with olive oil, toss and set aside.

Preheat a large skillet over medium-high heat with olive oil. Slice the eggplant into ½-inch-thick slices, then quarter each slice. Dredge in beaten eggs, then in rice flour and Italian breadcrumb mixture. Sauté in the skillet until golden brown and the centers are tender. Remove from skillet and set on paper towels.

In the same skillet you cooked the eggplant in, combine the garbanzo beans, corn, green chili, bell peppers and tomatoes. Season with salt and Italian breadcrumbs. Sauté until everything is thoroughly heated through.

In a large casserole dish, combine pasta and vegetable mix. Add shredded cheeses and toss together while hot. Serve immediately, or refrigerate and thoroughly reheat in the oven before serving.

Asparagus with Tangy Dijon sauce
Makes about 7 servings

1 ¼ lbs. asparagus spears
½ tsp. salt
¼ c. mayonnaise
1 tbsp. plus 1 tsp. Dijon mustard

2 tbsp. butter
¼ tsp. black pepper
1 tbsp. plus 1 tsp. cider vinegar
1 tsp. lemon juice

2 oz. bacon, cooked, drained and cut into little bits
2 hard-cooked eggs, finely chopped

Bring a large saucepan of salted water to a rolling boil. Snap off and discard the woody bases from the asparagus. Add the tops into the boiling water. Cook about 3 minutes or until tender, and drain.

Dijon sauce: Melt the butter over medium heat in a small saucepan. Stir in the salt, pepper, mayonnaise, mustard, vinegar and lemon juice. Heat thoroughly, stirring constantly.

Arrange the asparagus neatly on a serving platter, and drizzle with the sauce, reserving any excess sauce in a serving pitcher to be served alongside the platter.

Sprinkle the bacon and chopped eggs over the top, add additional salt and pepper if desired, and serve.

76

Dijon Agave Cream Sauce
Makes ½ to ¾ c.

½ c. evaporated milk
1 tbsp. plus 1 tsp. Dijon mustard
1 tbsp. agave nectar
2 tbsp. brown sugar
1 tsp. lemon pepper

Combine the evaporated milk, Dijon and agave in a small saucepan and whisk together. Add in the brown sugar, and whisk until everything is smooth over medium heat. *I like to taste the sauce at this point so that I can add more brown sugar if the sauce isn't as sweet as I want it that day.* Season with lemon pepper, stirring constantly over medium heat for 3-4 more minutes until smooth and bubbly.

Serve over your favorite steamed veggies... my favorites are green beans or asparagus!

This recipe doesn't yield much volume, but it does equal a lot of flavor!

Creamy Herb Mashed Potatoes
Serves 6

5 medium to large potatoes
½ c. heavy cream
1 stick (1/2 c.) melted butter
1 tsp. Italian Herb Blend Seasoning
Salt and Pepper to taste

Purple Mashed Potatoes
For an unexpected and colorful twist, I find it fun to use purple potatoes for this recipe! The vibrant purple color adds some fun to a regular meal, or really adds some flair to a special occasion! But don't worry... Their color doesn't change their flavor or how you need to cook them!

Preheat oven to 350°F.
Peel and wash potatoes. Put them in a large pot and cover completely with water. Boil on medium heat, uncovered, until fork-tender. Drain and put the potatoes into the bowl of a stand mixer. Mash potatoes in the stand mixer bowl using a paddle attachment. Using a whisk attachment, slowly mix in the melted butter and heavy cream. (You may add more melted butter and heavy cream if you desire even creamier potatoes.) Once the potatoes are nice and creamy, add in herb seasoning, salt, and pepper. Taste the mixture and adjust the seasoning as you wish. (Note: the herb seasoning flavor will develop over time, so don't overdo it!) Pour the mixture into an oven-safe baking dish. Cover with aluminum foil and put in a 350°F oven for 10 minutes, then serve.

Loaded Mashed Potatoes
Preheat the oven to 300°F. Prepare the Creamy Herb Mashed Potatoes as directed. Place the mixture into a 9x13 casserole dish, leveling the potatoes with a spatula. Sprinkle 2 c. shredded mild cheddar cheese and ½ c. freshly cooked bacon bits (approximately ½ lb. bacon, cooked until crispy and chopped into bits) over the mixture. Cover with aluminum foil and put in a 300°F oven until the cheese is melted.

Miss Coppertone - 1958

Wendy and her sisters were beach beauties that frequented the beaches of La Jolla, California, Waikiki, Hawaii and Guaymas, Mexico. At home they spent countless hours by the family pool, and as little girls they could swim before they could walk.

In 1958, Wendy won Miss Coppertone in Tucson, Arizona!

Homecoming Queen - 2013

Going into my Junior year of high school, I became a manager for our Varsity football team. As a Senior, I was made head manager and became even closer friends with the players. I took my responsibilities as a manager very seriously and made sure the team was well taken care of.

They completely surprised me when they elected me as the Homecoming Queen, and when I asked why they had, the boys simply replied, "because you deserve it!"

Thanks guys.

DOUGLAS BULLDOGS

Bulldog Cookies
Makes about 48 cookies

2 ¼ c. all-purpose flour
1 tsp. salt
1 tsp. baking soda
2 sticks (1 c.) butter, softened
¾ c. sugar
¾ c. packed brown sugar
1 tsp. vanilla extract
2 eggs

1 - 12 oz. bag white chocolate chips
1 - 12 oz. bag semi-sweet chocolate chips
1 - 12 oz. bag butterscotch chips

Preheat oven to 375°F.

In a medium bowl, combine flour, salt, and baking soda. Set aside.
In a mixer bowl, using a paddle attachment, beat together butter, sugar, brown sugar, and vanilla. Add in the eggs, one at a time, and beat just until everything is fairly well mixed. Add the flour mixture about half a cup at a time, leaving the mixer on low speed the entire time. Once all the flour is in, scrape down the sides of the bowl, mix again just long enough to incorporate the flour remnants, and check the bottom of the bowl so that there is no loose flour left. Add in all 3 bags of chips while the mixer is off. Turn the mixer on low speed to incorporate the chips, being careful not to let the dough come out over the sides of the bowl (these cookies are so jam-packed with goodies, the dough tends to get a little crazy and tries to come out of the bowl at this point!).
Lightly spray a baking sheet with nonstick cooking spray. Portion the cookies with your hands so that they are about the size of golf balls. Make sure the cookies have about an inch and a half to 2 inches between them when placing them on the tray. Bake at 375°F until the edges are light golden brown, about 8-10 minutes. Only let these cookies cool on the baking sheets for 3 or 4 minutes, then transfer them to cooling racks to cool completely.

Lineman Pasta
(This version should serve 6-8)

½ lb. bacon
8-oz. mild ground sausage
1 lb. bowtie pasta
½ stick (1/4 c.) melted butter, plus 1 tablespoon, softened
1 - 8 oz. pkg. cream cheese, softened
1 ½ c. fiesta blend finely shredded cheese
1 c. Italian breadcrumbs

In a large skillet, cook the bacon strips until cooked, but not totally crispy. Place on a paper towel to drain. Set aside.

In a large skillet, cook the sausage, stirring it around the pan and chopping it into small bits as it cooks. Place on a paper towel to drain. Set aside.

Cook the pasta as directed on the package, adding 1 tablespoon of softened butter to the pasta water before adding the pasta. Drain and pour the pasta into a large bowl. Drizzle in the half stick of melted butter and toss to coat the pasta. Add the cream cheese, bacon, sausage, and shredded cheese and mix well. Toss in the breadcrumbs.

Put in an oven-safe casserole dish, cover with aluminum foil and put into a 400°F oven for 10 minutes to let the cheeses melt. Remove from the oven and stir to make sure everything is well mixed and melted together.
Serve immediately, or cover again and keep in a warm oven until ready to serve.

Douglas Bulldogs
2013
Homecoming

Creamy Peanut Butter Sauce
Makes 2 ½ c.

4 tbsp. peanut butter
1 small 5-oz. can of evaporated milk
1 - 14 oz. can sweetened condensed milk
1 tbsp. brown sugar
1 tsp. Agave nectar

Combine all ingredients in a medium saucepan. Place over medium heat, stirring constantly, until smooth and creamy.
Store in the refrigerator. This sauce can be reheated in the microwave or on the stovetop.

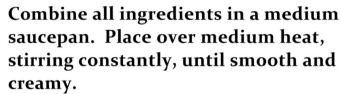

...arner, Malpai Ranch

Chocolate Ganache Dipping Sauce
Makes 1 ½ c.

2/3 c. heavy whipping cream
3 squares chocolate or white chocolate bark, chopped into small bits

In a medium saucepan over medium-high heat, bring the heavy cream to a boil, whisking often. Remove from heat and add the chopped bark. Do not stir together at this point! Wait 5 minutes, then stir to combine.

Twist: use a bag of butterscotch chips instead of the bark. The ganache will be thicker if you use chocolate, white chocolate, or butterscotch chips.

Warm Caramel Apple Sauce
Makes about 6 c.

1 stick (1/2 c.) butter
3 tablespoons cinnamon
1 tsp. vanilla

1 small 6-oz. can pineapple juice
1 c. packed brown sugar
5 large red apples, peeled and finely chopped

In a large skillet, melt the butter over medium-high heat. Add the pineapple juice, cinnamon, brown sugar and vanilla. Whisk vigorously until everything is well mixed, then add the chopped apples. Gently toss the apples to coat, then bring to a simmer. Once simmering, reduce the heat to medium and cover. Simmer for about 35 minutes, or until the apples are nice and tender and the liquid is almost syrupy. Serve warm.

Brandied Walnut Sauce
Makes 2 c.

1 ½ c. chopped walnuts
1 c. brown sugar, packed
½ c. orange juice
Cling peach halves

1/3 c. butter
2 tbsp. light corn syrup
¼ c. brandy

In a small skillet, sauté walnuts in butter over low heat for about 5 minutes, stirring constantly, until walnuts are very lightly browned. Cool. Combine sugar, corn syrup, and juice in a saucepan; simmer for 15 minutes. Add walnuts. Pour warm sauce over drained, cling peach halves. Heat brandy and pour over peaches and sauce. Flame.

Walnut Skillet Sauce
Makes 1 ¼ c.

¼ c. butter
1 c. coarsely chopped walnuts
1 c. semi-sweet chocolate pieces

Melt butter in heavy skillet. Add walnuts. Stir over moderate heat until nicely browned. Remove from heat. Add chocolate pieces and stir until melted and smooth.

Scrumptious Strawberry Amaretto Compote
Makes about 6 c.

1 qt. (1 box) whole strawberries, chopped
½ stick (1/4 c.) butter
½ c. sugar
½ c. brown sugar
½ c. Amaretto
1 tbsp. vanilla extract

In a large saucepan, melt the butter. Add in the sugar, brown sugar, amaretto and vanilla extract. Whisk ingredients together over medium heat until sugar is dissolved. Add in the strawberries, gently stir to coat with the cooking liquid, and cover. Reduce the heat to medium-low and cook until the strawberries are soft and the sauce is bubbly, stirring occasionally.

You can adjust the sugar measurements depending on how sweet or sour your strawberries are on a given day.

Warm Blackberry Compote
Makes about 5 c., depending on the size of the blackberries

4 c. blackberries, washed
1 c. sugar
4 tbsp. water

Pour the blackberries into a medium saucepan. Add in the sugar and water.

Turn the stove on medium heat, and stir the blackberry sugar mixture constantly until the sugar melts.

Continue to stir occasionally as the blackberries cook. The compote is ready once the blackberries have become soft.

Butterscotch Cashew Meringue Pie

¾ pkg. cinnamon graham crackers
¼ c. sugar
2/3 c. heavy whipping cream
¾ c. packed brown sugar
¼ tsp. salt
1 c. milk
1 tsp. vanilla extract
3 egg yolks
(reserve the whites in a separate bowl)

1 c. cashew pieces
¼ c. (1/2 stick) butter, melted
1 c. semi-sweet chocolate chips
¼ c. cornstarch
1 - 12 oz. can evaporated milk
3 tbsp. butter
1 recipe Brown Sugar Meringue

Preheat oven to 350°F.

In a food processor, combine the graham crackers, cashews and sugar. Pulse until the mixture turns to fine crumbs. Add the melted butter and continue to pulse until just combined. Pour into a 9" pie pan and use your fingers to press the mixture into the bottom and up the sides of the pan. Bake for 8 to 10 minutes at 350°F, then cool on a wire rack.

Prepare: Chocolate Layer

Pour the heavy whipping cream into a small saucepan and bring to a boil over medium-high heat, stirring almost constantly. Remove from the heat and add the chocolate chips, leaving them to sit 5 minutes before stirring. Once the 5 minutes have passed, stir the cream and chips together until the chocolate mixture is smooth. Pour the mixture over the cooled pie crust.

Prepare: Butterscotch Filling

Combine the brown sugar, cornstarch and salt in a medium saucepan. Whisk in the evaporated milk, egg yolks and milk until well combined. Cook over medium heat until thick and bubbly, stirring constantly. Remove from heat and stir in the butter and vanilla.
Cover and keep warm.

Prepare: Brown Sugar Meringue

Pour the warm butterscotch filling over the chocolate layer, and then heap the meringue on top, lightly spreading it into a dome shape that covers the edge of the crust and swirling the outside into soft peaks. Bake for 15 minutes, or until the meringue is firm and golden.
Cool on a wire rack for 1 hour then chill in the refrigerator, uncovered, for 4 to 6 hours before serving.

Don't Fence Me In

Those who ride before me talk of the wind in the trees, the roaring thunder and the black clouds breaking over the mountain peaks. The wildness of a storm. Nothing but the sound of the falling rain.

They ride through long winding canyons and bluffy ridges. I want to be there with them. In a vastness uninterrupted by civilization.
To hear the silence of the land, to see the sun beat down on a still landscape, and to savor the lonely freedom.

There's a javelina rooting at a mescal, a mule deer grazing on the beans of a cat claw bush. A bird screeching at the snake that's sneaking up on her nest. I heard a family of quail chatting as they went to roost. I wonder what they are saying...

I ride my mule "Tepini," and follow my grandpa... We'll chase lions together soon... I hope.
From him, I will learn to "whip and spur," to listen to the hounds and to strike a trot. I will learn the country, to follow the hounds, to rest my mule and to feel the spirit of the lion we are trailing. His tracks will tell us a story.

My grandma teaches me to "see" the birds, deer, and antelope and to know what they are. She shows me how to see the beauty and history in a rock, an arrowhead and a piece of pottery.

I want to see my reflection in a pond, next to the reflection of the trees, the sky, the openness. I want the chance to learn the lessons that even the smallest creatures of the wild have to teach.

My mom tells me how she and Warner ride good mules and of running lions off mountains. How they chase cows through thickets, roping wild cattle, crashing through brush, gritting their teeth and riding fast-running "rock-footed" ranch horses to get ahead of a herd of runaway cattle. They love it... I'm sure I will too.

To survive in the world that faces me, I will have to have an education in the classroom. I thank my Dad for passing his intellect on to me. Mom says that I will have to learn to take a second look at all situations before passing judgement. It will not just be what I learn from the wild, but from the combination of both worlds that will enable me to be fulfilled.

If all the beasts are gone and the land they live on is filled with civilization, the rangelands hold cattle no more, and the round-ups are no longer, those of us living this life will have a great loneliness of spirit.

I am six years old... Please don't fence me in...

My Mom and I wrote this when I was 6 years old for a gift to Warner and Wendy. It is framed in the Malpai Ranch house.

Sweet Potato Cranberry Sauté

1 ¼ c. apple juice
1 lb. sweet potatoes, peeled and cut into ¼-inch-thick slices (about 3 cups worth)
1 c. apple, coarsely chopped
½ c. dried cranberries
¼ c. maple syrup
¼ tsp. salt
¼ c. pecans, chopped
¼ c. brickle

In a large skillet, heat the apple juice until it's simmering. Add sliced sweet potatoes, making sure they're spread around evenly. Cook, covered, over medium-low heat for about 12-15 minutes, or until the potatoes are almost tender.

Stir in the apple, cranberries, maple syrup and salt. Continue cooking, covered, over low heat for an additional 3 - 5 minutes or until the apples are tender. Uncover and boil gently for about 4 more minutes until the liquid is thick like syrup.

Sprinkle the nuts and brickle over the top, and serve.

Mackenzie and "Clovis", J Bar A Ranch

Tequila Lime Cake

1 white cake mix
Zest of 2 large limes
1 - 3 oz. pkg. lime flavored Jello
1 c. sugar
1/2 c. butter
1/4 c. water
1/2 c. tequila

Preheat oven to 350° F.
Mix cake as directed adding lime zest and lime Jello.
Bake as directed. Remove from oven, let cool to room temperature.

Combine sugar, butter and water. Bring to a boil. Boil 15 minutes, stirring constantly. Stir in tequila and bring back to boil. Remove from heat.

Gently poke holes in top of cake with fork or thin knife.

Drizzle tequila mixture all over top of cake. It will soak in and saturate the cake.

Christmas Goodies

Five Minute Fudge
Makes about 25 pieces

1 - 12 oz. pkg. semi-sweet chocolate chips
2/3 c. sweetened condensed milk
1 tbsp. water
¾ c. pecans, chopped
1 tsp. vanilla extract

Line a baking sheet with parchment paper and set aside.

In a medium microwave-safe bowl, combine the chocolate chips, sweetened condensed milk and water. Microwave, uncovered, for 1 minute, then stir. Microwave another minute, uncovered, or until the chocolate is melted and the mixture is smooth when stirred every 30 seconds.

Stir in the nuts and vanilla. Drop the mixture by heaping spoonfulls onto the prepared baking sheet.

Chill in the refrigerator for about half an hour or until the fudge is firm.

Swirled Fudge
Makes about 70 bite-sized pieces

2 c. sugar
¼ tsp. salt
1 - 7 oz. jar marshmallow crème
¾ c. dark chocolate, chopped

1 c. evaporated milk
1 - 12 oz. pkg. white chocolate chips
2 ½ tsp. vanilla extract

Line a baking sheet (with edges) with foil, extending the foil over the edges of the pan. Butter the foil and set aside.

Butter the sides of a medium saucepan. In the pan, combine sugar, evaporated milk and salt. Cook over medium-high heat, stirring constantly, until the mixture boils. Reduce the heat to medium and continue cooking for 10 minutes, stirring often. Remove from heat. Add the white chocolate chips and marshmallow crème. Beat mixture vigorously with a whisk for 1 to 2 minutes until the mixture starts to thicken. Pour half of the mixture into a bowl.

For the white chocolate mixture: stir in 2 tablespoons of vanilla into the mixture in the bowl. Set aside.

For the dark chocolate mixture: add the chopped dark chocolate and the remaining vanilla to the mixture in the saucepan. Stir together until the dark chocolate melts and the mixture is smooth.

Immediately spread the dark chocolate mixture into the prepared pan and spread out evenly. Spoon the white chocolate mixture over the dark mixture in the pan, and swirl the two together using a toothpick, being careful not to completely mix them together. Allow to cool for 15 minutes before covering. Once covered, refrigerate for 4 to 5 hours until firm. Lift the fudge out of the pan using the foil edges, cut, and remove the foil from each piece.

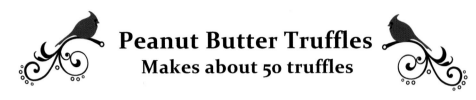

Peanut Butter Truffles
Makes about 50 truffles

2 c. sugar

1 stick (1/2 c.) butter

¾ c. creamy peanut butter

12-oz. dark or bittersweet chocolate, chopped

1 - 5 oz. can evaporated milk

2 c. mini marshmallows

½ tsp. vanilla

2 tsp. shortening

Butter the sides of a medium saucepan. In the pan, combine sugar, evaporated milk and butter. Cook and stir over medium-high heat until the mixture is boiling. Reduce the heat to medium and continue to boil the mixture at a moderate, steady rate for 12 minutes, stirring often. Remove from heat. Stir in the marshmallows, peanut butter and vanilla. Transfer the mixture into a large bowl. Chill for 45 minutes to an hour until the mixture is thick and can be molded easily.

Line a baking sheet with parchment paper. Using your hands, form the mixture into 1-inch balls and place them on the prepared baking sheet. Freeze for 15 minutes.

In a medium saucepan, combine the chopped chocolate and shortening. Cook over low heat, stirring constantly, until melted and smooth. Remove from heat. Dip each ball into the melted chocolate one at a time, rolling around to ensure even coating. Use a fork to pick up the balls and allow the extra chocolate to drip off before placing them back onto the prepared baking sheet or a wire rack set over parchment paper. Let stand until the chocolate is set.

Cinnamon Pistachio Brittle
Makes about 10 oz. of candy

½ c. sugar
½ c. light corn syrup
1 c. pistachios
1 tbsp. butter
½ tsp. baking soda
½ tsp. cinnamon
½ tsp. vanilla

Line a baking sheet (with edges) with foil, extending the foil over the edges of the pan. Butter the foil and set aside.

In a medium microwave-safe bowl, combine the sugar and corn syrup. Microwave, uncovered, for 3 minutes, stirring twice. Stir in the nuts and butter. Microwave, uncovered, for 2 or 3 minutes until the mixture just turns a light golden color, stirring after 1 minute and again every 30 seconds after that.

Note: The mixture continues to cook and turns more golden when removed from the microwave.

Quickly whisk in the baking soda, cinnamon and vanilla, continuing to whisk constantly. Immediately pour the mixture onto the prepared baking sheet. Spread the mixture out as thin as possible. Allow the mixture to cool completely before breaking into pieces and serving or storing.

Soft Chocolate Toffee Bars
Makes about 40 bars

2 c. flour
½ tsp. cinnamon
1 tsp. vanilla
1 c. milk chocolate chips

1 c. packed brown sugar
2 sticks (1 c.) butter, softened
¾ c. pecans, chopped
½ c. toffee/brickle bits

Preheat oven to 350°F.

Line a 9x13 baking pan with foil, extending the ends of the foil completely over the edges of the pan. Grease the foil with butter and set aside.

In a large bowl, stir together the flour, brown sugar and cinnamon. Add the butter and vanilla, and beat with an electric mixer on low speed until the mixture forms coarse crumbs. Stir in the pecans and half of the chocolate chips. Spread the mixture into the prepared pan and press down firmly.

Bake at 350°F for 25 to 30 minutes or until golden brown. Remove the pan from the oven and sprinkle bars with the remaining chocolate chips. Let stand on a wire rack for 5 minutes so that the newly added chips soften. After the 5 minutes are up, spread the chocolate pieces all over the bars and immediately top with the brickle bits.

Let the pan cool completely on the wire rack, allowing the bars to cool completely before cutting them. Use the foil edges to lift the bars out of the pan, and then peel off the foil from each bar after cutting.

Chocolate Cherry Cashew Clusters
Makes about 35 clusters

3 c. whole salted cashews
1 - 12 oz. pkg. semi-sweet chocolate chips
4-oz. (about 1/3 of a 12-oz. bag) milk-chocolate chips
1 c. dried sweet cherries, chopped
½ of a 20-oz. pkg. of white bark, cut into 2-inch chunks

Watch and check the chocolate in the slow cooker every 15 minutes or so to avoid scorching.

Place almonds in the bottom of a 3.5 or 4-quart slow cooker. Layer the semi-sweet and milk chocolate chips over the almonds. Sprinkle in the chopped cherries and top with the bark chunks.

Cover and cook on the low-heat setting for 1 ½ to 2 hours, or until the chocolate is melted just enough to stir everything together.

Meanwhile, line 2 baking sheets with mini paper baking cups; set aside.

Carefully remove the slow cooker lid and stir the mixture to ensure that everything is combined.
Using a tablespoon, drop the mixture into the paper baking cups.

Chill in the refrigerator for about an hour, or until the chocolate is set.

Warner

Grant Watkins

Diego Suarez

Wendy

Livin' La Vida Loca... Translation: livin' the crazy life!

Our lives are crazier now more than ever, with our work force narrowing down to three main characters: Warner, Mom and myself. We continue to ranch the two family-owned ranches and have the grazing lease on a third. Warner and Mom still guide hunts all winter for lion, they take a deer hunter or two and guide through spring javelina season.

Thanks to friends and neighbors, we usually have someone close by to help out with the heavy lifting and longer days. Our dear friend Carrie Krentz helps Mom with the bookkeeping and making the transition after losing Wendy and all that she did for the business end of the ranching and hunting.

Our Malpai Ranch is located on the Mexican Border. Our southern boundary is the border itself, so we are on the front lines of the border security issues, illegal immigration and drug trafficking. It is something that you learn to live with and in the process, we play host to Congressional tours and media inquiries, smugglers and border security forces.

Drought has plagued this region for years. However this year (2014) we had what is called a 1000-year-flood, caused by 6.35 inches of rain in two and a half days. Water flooded places that have never been under water!

I have been allowed to venture into my own interests including raising market and carcass steers and market hogs, participating in the FFA, managing sports teams at our high school, venturing into my passion for culinary and further pursuing my interests in the beef industry. Having graduated from high school in May 2014, I am not heading off to college, but rather staying near to help with the ranches and following my own business interests for awhile. We'll see where the road takes us in the future... Here's to the ride!

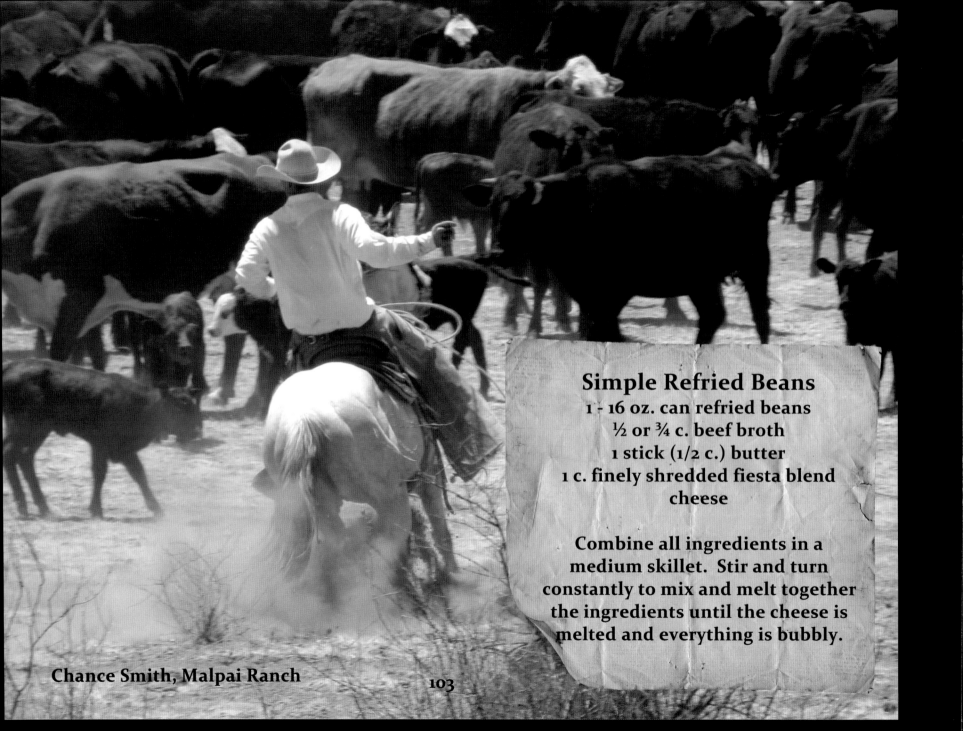

Simple Refried Beans

1 - 16 oz. can refried beans
½ or ¾ c. beef broth
1 stick (1/2 c.) butter
1 c. finely shredded fiesta blend cheese

Combine all ingredients in a medium skillet. Stir and turn constantly to mix and melt together the ingredients until the cheese is melted and everything is bubbly.

Chance Smith, Malpai Ranch

A Twist on Tostadas

Serves 4 - 6

1 lb. ground beef
1 - 25 oz. can white hominy, drained, rinsed, and chopped
1 - 4 oz. can diced green chile
2 strips roasted red bell peppers, diced
1 c. low-sodium beef broth
½ c. mild green taco sauce
1 pkg. Lowery's or McCormick's taco seasoning
½ tsp. lemon pepper

Cook the ground beef in a large skillet and drain in a strainer. Return the meat to the pan, and add the hominy, diced green chile and roasted red peppers. In a bowl, mix the beef broth, mild green taco sauce, taco seasoning and lemon pepper. Pour over meat mixture and stir everything together. Bring to a simmer over medium heat and let simmer for 10-15 minutes to allow the flavors to become well incorporated. Drain any left over liquid.
To assemble your tostada, I recommend spreading a layer of refried beans onto the shell first. Then add your meat, lightly pressing it into the beans. Add your favorite ingredients, including shredded lettuce, diced tomatoes, sliced black olives, chopped avocadoes or fresh guacamole, salsa, shredded cheese, diced onions, jalapenos.... The options are endless!

My dad, Kerry Kimbro, hailing from Houston, Texas! A true food connoisseur.

Mom met Dad at a Ben Johnson Pro-Celebrity Rodeo. Mom was a celebrity contestant and Dad was providing rope horses for the contestants.

Dad was born and raised in the Houston, Texas region, and grew up as a calf roper and team roper. He has spent his career working for electric power companies, first as a Journeyman Lineman and in later years as a Construction Maintenance Coordinator.

No longer roping and nearing retirement, Dad stands by and supports us as we spin around him with all of our endeavors.

It is a sure bet that Dad knows good food and he can definitely cook, no doubt picking up those skills from his mom, my grandma, Mimi!

Albondigas
Serves 6

Flatten out 1 lb. of raw, lean ground beef on a clean work surface until it is about 1/2-inch-thick. Sprinkle with salt, pepper, lemon pepper, 2 pinches of fine oregano leaves and garlic powder.
Roll back together and knead. Form 1-inch meatballs. Fry in a dry skillet until done.

In a large pot, mix together 1 - 32 oz. carton of beef broth, 1/3 medium onion-chopped, 3 celery stalks-chopped, 5 cubes of cilantro seasoning and 2 cubes of beef bouillon.
Boil till celery and onions are tender and sink to the bottom of the liquid.

In a separate pot, boil 2 Boil-in-the-Bag rice bags, 10-15 minutes until almost tender.
Add meat to broth with celery and onions, plus 2 - 4 oz. cans diced green chili and 1 qt. water.
Heat and bring back to a boil. Add in the rice and serve.

Dad's Hot Potato Salad
Serves 6

5 large potatoes, peeled and
boiled
4 1/2 tbsp. mustard
2 tbsp. mayonaise
3 tbsp. dill pickle relish
1 whole dill pickle, diced
Salt and Pepper to taste

Peel and boil the potatoes.
Mash to a creamy state while hot.
Add in all other ingredients.
Mix well and serve while hot.

Optional:
Add in one finely chopped stalk of celery
and/or
1/4 finely chopped white onion

My cool step-brother Kyle
put his time in the US Air Force,
stationed at Luke Air Force Base in
Phoenix, Arizona and Kunsan Air
Force Base in South Korea.

He is attending college now at
Tarleton State University,
Stephenville, Texas, majoring in
Applied Sciences of Business.

My step-brother, Kyle

Carisa's Coconut Meringue Pie

Combine 1 c. sugar, 1/2 c. cornstarch and 1/8 tsp. salt in a saucepan. Whisk in 1 can of coconut milk, plus enough regular whole milk to make 3 c. of liquid total, until combined. Cook over medium heat until thick, and then continue to cook for 1-2 minutes after mixture begins to bubble. Remove from heat.

In a large saucepan, beat 4 egg yolks and add ½ c. of the hot filling mixture, stirring constantly. Continue to add the filling mixture, ½ c. at a time, whisking quickly until well blended so that you don't overheat the yolks. Cook an additional 3 minutes over medium heat, whisking often to prevent scorching. Remove from heat.

Thoroughly whisk 4 tbsp. softened butter and 2 tsp. vanilla extract into the hot filling mixture, then fold in 1 1/2 c. shredded coconut. Pour the filling into one baked 9" pie crust. Add one recipe of meringue in a heap, making sure to cover the edges and build soft peaks on the outside. Bake at 350°F just until the meringue browns. Cool before serving so that the pie has time to set up. To store, cover and refrigerate.

My step-sister, Carisa, is a Captain in the Texas Army National Guard and a Bronze Star recipient! She served as Company Executive Officer in Operation Enduring Freedom, stationed at Bagram Air Base, Afghanistan; and as Company Commander at Balad Air Base, Iraq, in Operation Iraqi Freedom. She is currently serving as Bravo Company Chinook 2-149 GSAB Company Commander.

Meringue

Stir 1 1/2 tbsp. cornstarch into slightly more than ½ c. cold water and heat on the stovetop until thick. Remove from heat and set aside to cool at room temperature.

In a stand mixer on medium-high speed, beat 6 egg whites until frothy. Continue beating on medium speed, and slowly add 1 1/2 c. sugar in ½ c. increments to allow the sugar to dissolve. After the sugar has dissolved and the meringue makes soft peaks, add the cornstarch mixture a tbsp. at a time on medium-high speed until stiff peaks form.

Make this recipe while your pie filling mixture is cooking!

Kelly's Sweet Cookies, Cherries, Cream, and Strawberries

Raw, precut chocolate chip cookie dough (enough for about 24, 2-inch round cookies)
2 - 15 oz. cans pitted dark sweet cherries
2 - 8 oz. pkgs. cream cheese
1 - 14 oz. can sweetened condensed milk
1 small 8-oz. container Cool Whip
12 strawberries, maybe more or less depending on their size

Grease a 9x13 baking dish. Preheat the oven to 350°F.
Place the raw cookie dough in the bottom of the pan, making sure each cookie is touching. Bake until cooked, and remove from the oven.
Drain half of the juice off of the cherries, and pour the cherries and remaining juice into a food processor. Pulse to chop into tiny pieces. Spread the chopped cherry mixture over the warm cookie crust.
Mix together the cream cheese and sweetened condensed milk in a stand mixer, whipping until lumps disappear. Fold in the Cool Whip. Spread this mixture over the chopped cherries.
Layer fresh cut strawberries over the top, chill and serve.

Bonus note: the extra juice that is strained off of the cherries makes a great addition to orange juice the next morning!

THE PERFECT MID-SIZE GAME RIFLE

Ruger's Mini Thirty

Some guns go along like a good companion on a hunt, adding to the experience only hunters know as they wait or stalk through the woods and mountains on a fresh, clear day. The new Ruger Mini Thirty is the ideal rifle to bring out the most in the hands of the new shooter and experienced hunter alike. Lightweight, fast handling, with little recoil, the Mini Thirty is chambered for the modern 7.62 × 39mm cartridge. Designed for use with telescopic sights, the Mini Thirty incorporates Ruger's low profile scope-mounting system. Designed with the needs of *today's* shooter foremost in the mind of Ruger engineers, the Mini Thirty is made possible by Ruger's advanced manufacturing techniques.

 STURM, RUGER & Company, Inc.

49 Lacey Place
Southport, Connecticut 06490

Free instruction manuals for all Ruger firearms are available upon request.

1988

Mom became "The Ruger Girl" in 1988 because she was a 5th generation rancher and a 3rd generation hunting guide. They wanted someone to reepresent family and tradition... She is still representing, 27 years later!

2014

Kelly Glenn-Kimbro

THE RUGER® GUNSITE
SCOUT RIFLE

The one rifle to have if you could have only one.

A scout rifle is the perfect "go-to" gun for multi-purpose use: hunting, ranching, personal defense and emergency response. It is the perfect lightweight, hard hitting, do-it-all, magazine-fed, bolt-action rifle.

.COM/SCOUTRIFLE

® RUGER

Lucky enough to travel!

This recipe is from Vito's Chophouse in Orlando, Florida.
The traveling that has resulted from Mom's "run" as "The Ruger Girl" has led to Mom and I getting to visit some great cities in the US, eating in awesome restaurants and getting to make some very special friends in the firearms industry.

I know for certain that Mom has treasured her time with Sturm, Ruger & Co., Inc.
The faith that Tom Ruger had in 1988 when he braved the image of a woman representing his family's firearms manufacturing company has been well appreciated by our family.

Mom loves her work and her fans and the honor to represent this American company.

Vito's Chop House
Orlando, Florida
Shrimp Portabello Bake

Layer 1: Cracker Mix
Mix and layer in the bottom of a baking dish: saltines, butter, onions, bacon, mayo, fresh dill, 151 rum, liquid eggs.

Layer 2: Portabello
Scrape out mushrooms. Marinate the mushroom in Italian dressing. Place in dish on cracker mix.

Layer 3: Creamed Spinach
Spinach, heavy whipping cream, garlic.

Layer 4: Shrimp
Place large raw shelled shrimp on top of spinach layer.
Bake 18 minutes at 350°F. Remove and top with hollandaise sauce and cheddar cheese. Bake 2 more minutes. Serve.

Sweet Water Prawns with Roasted Red Peppers and Fresh Basil
Serves 8

24 large shrimp
½ tsp. dried thyme (or 1 tsp. chopped fresh thyme)
4 tbsp. olive oil
2 garlic clove, finely chopped
Salt and Pepper
½ red bell pepper, chopped
½ yellow bell pepper, chopped
2 tbsp. fresh basil leaves

Place shrimp in a plastic bowl or bag with thyme, olive oil, garlic, salt and pepper to taste. Shake and mix to thoroughly coat the shrimp. Refrigerate one hour. Sauté the bell peppers in olive oil with basil leaves until the peppers are almost tender. Stir in shrimp and marinade. Sauté 8 to 10 minutes until shrimp is cooked. Serve immediately with toasted French bread.

Now and then we have ranch guests that are not keen on beef...go figure!
So, for one special occasion Mom created this dish and it was a hit.
No doubt she also served beef the same night, because Warner is a cattleman who stays true to the industry and beef is what's for his dinner!

Chiricahua Mountains, SE Arizona

Diamond A, Animas Mountains, New Mexico

Malpai Borderlands Group (MBG)

An "event" that changed the lives of Warner, Wendy and Mom was the creation of an organization that would eventually become an icon in the West.
The idea took shape on the front porch of our Malpai Ranch house and with Wendy as the office coordinator, an office was established in our ranch house for the next 25 years.

The Malpai Borderlands Group goal statement reads: "Our goal is to restore and maintain natural processes that create and protect a healthy, unfragmented landscape to support a diverse, flourishing community of human, plant and animal life in our borderlands region. Together, we will accomplish this by working to encourage profitable ranching and other traditional livelihoods which will sustain the open space nature of our land for generations to come."

The group was formed to preserve ranching heritage and wildlife corridors, and blend the common ground of science and practicality. The group blends the efforts of ranchers, businessmen, scientists, biologists and Federal and State Agencies. Contributors and participants hail from the greater United States, Africa, Mongolia, Kenya and Argentina, to name a few. MBG has been on the leading edge of conservation easements, unlikely collaborations and grassbanking.

Many meals have been prepared in our kitchen for hundreds of people through the years. These events ranged from Board meetings to ranching workshops. Fire on the landscape, Mexican Border issues, grass banking, scholarships, and the many methods of enhancing the landscape whether for wildlife or cattle have graced the agendas.

The MBG has brought together a wide range of folks through the years. They have all shared a good meal. Many times, this has cemented a deal, finalized an idea or raised much needed funding.

One such event was a fundraising dinner that Mom coordinated and produced in the Gray Ranch barn. She took an extremely remote location, a barn that is over 100 years old, a rented load of sterling and china, a 48-foot tablecloth, antlers, candles, Indian pots, filet mignon, "Robin's stuffed mushrooms," good wine, a hand-picked hardworking crew and pulled off a historical intimate dinner for 48 people in the middle of a vast, awe-inspiring wilderness.

The funds raised from this event would insure the continuation of the MBG goals and a new level of conservation easements.

Mexican-Style Pot Roast
Serves 40 people

20 lb. sirloin tip roast	6 garlic cloves	2 red peppers
2 green peppers	2 lg. onions	4 - 16 oz. cans tomato puree
1 c. red wine vinegar	4 tbsp. sugar	8 tsp. salt
4 tsp. oregano		

Saute garlic in 1 c. olive oil. Pour flavored oil over roasts. Cover roasts with peppers, onions, tomato pure, red wine vinegar, sugar, salt and oregano, plus 1 c. water. Roast at 350°F, turning once every hour. If the meat starts out thawed, cook for 3 hours. If the meat starts out frozen, cook 4 to 5 hours.

Lemon Cake with Chocolate Almond Frosting

Bake a lemon cake as instructed on the box. Turn out of the pan and cool.
In a food processor, blend together:
1 - 12 oz. pkg. chocolate chips
1 c. chopped or slivered almonds
2 tsp. cinnamon
2 tsp. almond flavor
2 tbsp. margarine, softened
Pour in enough canned milk to make a frosting consistency. If too thin, thicken with powdered sugar.
Frost the cake. Note that the frosting will harden.

Meringue Crust
Serves 4

Beat 3 egg whites and ¼ tsp. cream of tarter until frothy. Gradually add in ¾ c. sugar, beating at high speed till sugar is dissolved and stiff, glossy peaks form.

Butter bottom and sides of one 9-inch pie pan.

Spread meringue evenly over bottom and sides of pie pan.

Bake at 250°F for 1 hour.
Turn oven off and leave meringue in oven 2 more hours. Let cool in a dry place.

Filling Variations

LIME: Beat together 1 can sweetened condensed milk and ½ c. lime juice till smooth and slightly thickened. Fold in 8 oz. Cool Whip. Spatula spread into meringue crust and chill.

ALMOND: replace lime juice with 2 tsp. almond flavoring.

Try not to make this recipe when the weather is humid.

Southwest Veggie Stew
over rice
Serves 8

1 - 15 oz. can cannellini beans, drained
1 - 15 oz. can garbanzo beans, drained
1 - 11 oz. can white corn, drained
1 - 11 oz. can yellow corn, drained
Shredded carrots
Chopped zucchini
2 - 4 oz. cans diced green chili
1 chopped onion
Asparagus, diced large
2 chicken bouillon cubes
1 clove garlic, minced
1 tsp. ground cumin
1 tbsp. olive oil
2 plus c. grated cheese
1-2 tbsp. chopped fresh cilantro

Combine beans, corn and green chili. Set aside.
Steam carrots, zucchini and asparagus till crisp tender.
Saute onion, garlic, cumin and oil.
Dissolve bouillon cube in 2-3 c. water.
Combine all of the above and chopped cilantro.
Bring to a boil.
Serve over rice.

Meatloaf for a Crowd
Serves 30

17 lbs. ground beef
6 slices of toast, crumbs (food processor)
1 ½ c. crushed shredded wheat (food processor)
4 - 6 oz. cans veggie juice cocktail
8-10 eggs
1 lg. onion and 1-2 lg. green peppers (both diced in a food
processor)
1 can milk (optional) for moisture
4 plus tbsp. Worcestershire sauce
2 tsp. garlic powder
4 tsp. salt
2 ½ tsp. pepper
4 tsp. rosemary leaves
2 ½ tsp. powdered thyme

Mix all ingredients together. Press into one or two
casserole dishes based on availability.

Bake at 350° F for 1 ½ hours.

Baked Indian Soup
Serves 30 people

½ gallon corn
½ or 1 lg. onion
4 tomatoes
½ gallon hominy
2 small cans sliced olives
2 lg. cans diced green chili
8 medium squash
Butter
Salt & Pepper

Combine all ingredients and place in extra large casserole dish.

Heat and mix together 3 c. heavy whipping cream with 1 -20 oz. can green enchilada sauce.
Sauté 2-3 cloves grated garlic, 1 onion and 1 - 4 oz. can diced green chili
in oil.
Stir in cream mixture and salt to taste. Pour over vegetable mixture. Top with grated cheddar or jack cheese and bake until squash is tender and mixture is bubbly.

Mediterranean Pork
Serves 10 - 12

10 lbs. pork loin
1 - 16 oz. jar Italian dressing
1/2 of 14-oz. can Italian seasoned diced tomatoes
1 - 6 oz. can chopped olives
4 lg. strips of roasted red bell pepper, diced
1/2 medium size onion, chopped

Preheat oven to 350° F.

Layer pork with all ingredients in a
casserole dish.

Cover witha lid or aluminum foil.

Bake 2.5 to 3 hours.

Chapter 6
Insight from the Outside

Diamond A Ranch
SW New Mexico

Our cattle ranches have always played multiple roles in the lives of many.

Besides beef production, we have guided mountain lion and deer hunts for over 60 years, hosted paying ranch guests for over 50 years and have been the jumping off point for organizations like the Cowbelles and the Malpai Borderlands group.

Our ranches have played host to hundreds of guests ranging from city kids needing to have the homegrown ranch experience to ranchers from across the nation, Alaska and Hawaii, Sonora, Chihuahua, and Cohuilla, Mexico, and countries including Argentina and Canada. Guests have included Maasai herdsmen from Kenya, Mongolian horsemen, wildlife biologists from the base of Mt. Kilimanjaro in Africa, a coues deer hunter from Austria, college professors, Congressmen, Senators, Arizona Governor Jan Brewer, (and the accompanying Secret Service and Capital Police), teachers, State and Federal agency folks, botanists, biologists, border patrol, illegal aliens (good and bad), ranchers, farmers, hunters (and anti-ranchers and anti-hunters), feedlot owners, cattle buyers, movie stars and a large treasured group of really good friends.

A large ranch meal is always an ice breaker and eating is a common bond. Recipes are shared, stories told, memories relived, ideas born and developed and problems solved.

This chapter has a few of the recipes that have been shared by our friends, neighbors and guests.

Streusel Topping for
Cinnamon Chocolate Streusel Cake

1 - 12 oz. pkg. semi-sweet chocolate chips
1 - 12 oz. pkg. cinnamon baking chips
1 large egg yolk
7 tbsp. salted butter, at room temperature
1 c. all-purpose flour

In a food processor, pulse the cinnamon and chocolate chips until they are the consistency of coarse crumbs.
Remove half and set aside for the batter.
Add the egg yolk, butter and flour to the food processor bowl with half of the cinnamon chocolate crumbs. Pulse just until everything is thoroughly combined - it should look crumbly, not processed to a paste. Set aside.

Personally, I like the cake most when it is still slightly warm.
Vanilla, caramel, or cinnamon flavored ice cream pair well with this cake.
Storage: Tightly wrapped, the finished cake keeps great for several days, though you may want to warm pieces at a very low temperature in the oven before serving.

Cinnamon Chocolate Streusel Cake
Serves 12

1 ¾ c. all-purpose flour
1 ¼ tsp. baking powder
1 - 8 oz. pkg. cream cheese, at room temperature
1 c. unsalted butter, at room temperature
2/3 c. granulated sugar
4 large eggs, at room temperature
Powdered sugar for dusting the cake

Preheat oven to 350°F. Spray a 9x13 baking pan with cooking spray.
Sift together the flour and baking powder in a medium bowl and set aside.
Combine the cream cheese, butter and granulated sugar in the bowl of a stand mixer and beat until light and fluffy, 2 to 3 minutes. Add the eggs one at a time, beating until each one is thoroughly incorporated. Add the sifted flour mixture. Scrape down the sides of the bowl and beat for 1 minute, just until the flour is incorporated. Stir the reserved cinnamon chocolate crumbs from the streusel mixture into the batter.
Scrape the batter into the prepared pan and smooth the top.
Sprinkle the streusel topping evenly over the batter. Bake in the center of the oven until the cake is springy, the edges have just begun to pull away from the sides of the pan, and a toothpick inserted into the center of the cake comes out clean, 35 to 40 minutes. Cool on a wire rack, cut into squares and serve dusted with powdered sugar.

Diego Suarez

Robin's Stuffed Mushrooms
Makes about 30 mushrooms

1 ½ lbs. (approx. 30) medium
mushrooms
½ lb. pork sausage
½ c. shredded mozzarella cheese
¼ c. Italian seasoned bread crumbs

Preheat oven to 450°F.
Clean mushrooms and remove
stems. Chop the stems, and set
aside the caps.
Cook and drain the sausage.
Reserve 2 tbsp. of the sausage
grease in the pan and use to sauté
stems until tender, about 10
minutes. In a medium bowl, stir
together sausage, stems, cheese
and crumbs. Fill mushroom caps
with mixture. Bake 15 minutes in a
pan with sides.

Robin Brekhus: a great friend. She owns the Avenue
Bed and Breakfast in Douglas, Arizona. Robin has
cowboyed for us, helped work cattle and lion hunted
with us through the years.

Chicken Salad

1 pre-roasted whole chicken, pulled off
the bone and chopped
2 c. sweet grapes, cut into quarters
1/2 c. sliced almonds, slightly roasted
4-6 tbsp. mayonnaise
2 stalks of celery, chopped
1 whole apple, peeled and chopped
Pepper to taste

Mix all ingredients together and use for
salads or sandwiches.

Rick and Heather Knight visit the ranches twice a year.
Heather is originally from Australia and works for
The Nature's Conservancy in Colorado.
Rick is a Professor of Wildlife Conservation at
Colorado State University, with a particular interest in
ranching and ranch families.
They come stay at the J Bar A and work for us hauling
rock for erosion structures, moving cattle, branding,
mixing cement, etc! Their zest for life is unmatched!

Heather's Wild Bird Appetizers

Recipe given to Heather Knight by Jed Meunier, the great-grandson of Aldo Leopold.

Breast meat of dove, quail or duck
Thousand Island dressing
Bacon
Roasted Green Chiles or Jalapenos
Wooden Skewers

Take the breasts of the bird and cut them into bite-sized pieces. Marinate the meat in a generous amount of Thousand Island dressing for at least 1 hour, and up to 2 hours or so for darker meat.

Meanwhile, soak wooden skewers in water. This will prevent them from burning on the grill or under the broiler.

Cut strips of bacon and fresh roasted green chiles. You can use jalapeños for more spice, if you desire.
Lay out each bacon strip. On top, place a strip of green chile or jalapeño, then place the marinated pieces of meat on top. Wrap the bacon and green chile around the meat and skewer it. Leave gaps between each bundle. Cook on the grill or under the broiler until the bacon starts to crisp and the bird meat is cooked. Turn carefully during cooking by grabbing the skewers with tongs to ensure even cooking.

Eat them right off the grill!

This also works well for pork!

Summer Cowboys

"Good Hands"   Good friends!

Connor Mullins
Santa Fe, New Mexico

Grant Watkins
Douglas, Arizona

Linda's Cranberry Salad

1 pkg. fresh cranberries
2 c. sugar
1 c. chopped celery
1 c. chopped pecans
½ pt. heavy whipping cream, whipped
Pecan halves, for garnish

½ c. pineapple juice
1 small 3-oz. box strawberry Jello
1 c. crushed pineapple, drained
1 - 13 oz. jar marshmallow cream
1 - 8 oz. pkg. cream cheese, whipped

Cook the cranberries in the pineapple juice until the skins pop. Add sugar, Jello, nuts, pineapple, and celery. Stir and let set until thickened.

Fold together the whipped cream, marshmallow cream, and whipped cream cheese. Once thoroughly mixed, place over Jello mixture. Garnish with pecan halves.

Linda's Broccoli Puff
Serves 6-8

1 - 10 oz. pkg. frozen broccoli cuts
1 - 10.75 oz. can cream of mushroom soup
½ c. shredded cheddar cheese
¼ c. bread crumbs

¼ c. milk
¼ c. mayonnaise
1 egg, beaten
1 tbsp. butter

Linda and her family are pillars of the community, constantly fundraising for cancer victims and sports teams! With a deep faith and true grit, she is a woman to be admired.

Cook frozen broccoli according to package directions, omitting the salt that the package directions calls for. Drain thoroughly. Place broccoli cuts in 10 x 6 x 1 ½ baking dish. Gradually add milk, mayo and beaten egg to soup mixture, stirring till well blended. Pour over broccoli in baking dish, top with bread crumbs, butter and cheese. Bake at 350°F until firm, bubbly and slightly toasted on top.

Jenn's Brownies

Jenn Shelton is a great gal, tons of fun, and loves to bake!

1/3 c. unsweetened cocoa powder
2 tsp. instant espresso
½ c. plus 2 tbsp. boiling water
2-oz. unsweetened chocolate, chopped
4 tbsp. unsalted butter, melted
½ c. plus 2 tbsp. vegetable oil

2 large eggs, plus 2 large egg yolks
2 tsp. vanilla extract
½ tsp. almond extract
2½ c. sugar
1¾ c. all-purpose flour
approximately ½ tsp. coarse sea salt

1 to 1 ½ c. dark chocolate chips (however much you desire)

Put oven rack in lowest position and preheat to 350°F. Line a 9x13 baking pan with foil, leaving a 2-inch overhang on all sides. Spray with nonstick cooking spray.
Using the whisk attachment on low to medium speed, whisk the cocoa, espresso powder and boiling water until smooth. Add unsweetened chocolate and whisk until chocolate is melted. Add melted butter and oil, and whisk just until combined. Add eggs, yolks, vanilla extract and almond extract. Continue to whisk until smooth, then whisk in sugar until fully incorporated. Add flour and salt and mix just until combined. Remove bowl from mixer, scrape down sides with a spatula, and fold in chocolate chips. Pour batter into pan and bake 30 to 35 minutes. Put pan on wire rack to cool, then cut into squares and serve.
If using a glass dish, remove from pan after ten minutes using foil as a lift,; for all other pans, remove brownies after cool to touch, about 1 hour. Either way, finish cooling on a wire rack.

Carrie's Fudge

1 ½ c. sugar
1 - 5 oz. can evaporated milk (2/3 c.)
3 c. semisweet chocolate chips
2 c. nuts, coarsely chopped (walnuts or pecans)

½ c. margarine (blue-bonnet works best)
1 - 7 oz. jar marshmallow crème
½ tsp. vanilla extract

Lightly grease a jelly roll pan. Heat the sugar, margarine, milk and marshmallow crème in heavy 3-quart pan over medium heat until the mixture boils, stirring constantly. Boil and stir for 5 minutes. Add the chocolate chips and vanilla extract, stirring until the chips are melted. Stir in the nuts. Immediately spread into prepared pan. Refrigerate overnight. Cut into 1-inch squares. Store in an airtight container in the refrigerator. Makes 4 pounds.

Carrie Krentz was Wendy's port in the storm when it came to office affairs, & she continues to be a lifesaver for us!

Moving cattle from Malpai to Rocker M

Carmen Medlin's Homemade Butter Pecan or Butter Brickle Ice Cream

Makes 6 qt.

6 eggs
2 c. sugar
13-oz. Cool Whip
2 tsp. vanilla
¾ gallon whole milk
3 boxes butter pecan instant pudding mix
¾ c. crushed heath bars or pecans

Mix the eggs, sugar, cool whip, vanilla, whole milk and instant pudding mix together. Pour into 6-quart old fashioned ice cream maker. Pack around center can with ice and ice cream salt. Turn on machine and let churn, checking periodically for the desired frozen state.
Add in pecans or crushed heath bars.
Churn one more minute.
Empty container and freeze or eat!

141

Carmen's Homemade Vanilla Ice Cream
Makes 1 gallon

6 eggs

1 - 12 oz. can evaporated milk

2 ½ c. sugar

2 tbsp. vanilla extract

Beat together the eggs and sugar, and then add the evaporated milk and vanilla. Pour into the ice cream maker container, and add milk to the container until the liquid reaches the proper level as stated in your machine's handbook. Pack with ice and ice cream salt and churn until desired consistency is reached.

Carmen and Geraldine Medlin are long-time friends and hunting clients of the Glenn's. Through the years, Geraldine's dad, sisters, brother-in-laws, sons and employees all killed lions with Marvin, Warner and Mom.
They hail from Sullivan, Missouri and occasionally they still drop in to quail hunt.

Crockpot Fudge

From Cynthia Bohmfalk, my 2nd grade teacher and one of our best friends who always rises to the occasion!

1 pkg. chocolate bark
1 box german chocolate bar
3 c. cashews or peanuts or almonds

1 pkg. white chocolate bark
1 - 12 oz. pkg. milk chocolate chips

Combine ingredients in a slow cooker. Cook on low for 3 hours, stirring occasionally to blend. Drop onto wax paper with a teaspoon. Allow to air harden for a couple hours. If it's warm weather, you can refrigerate or freeze to harden, and freeze to store them. Makes about 75-80 pieces.

Beverly Taylor's Swedish Delight
(Cynthia's sweet Mom)
Serves 10-12

1/2 to 3/4 pkg. vanilla wafers, crushed fine
2 squares bitter chocolate
½ c. butter
2 c. powdered sugar
3 egg yolks
Salt
1 c. pecans or walnuts, chopped fine
3 egg whites, beaten stiff
Vanilla ice cream

Line bottom of a 9x13 pan with crushed
wafers. Melt the chocolate and butter, then
add the powdered sugar, egg yolks, salt and
nuts. Let cool.
Once cooled, fold in the egg whites. *I
double this because I like a thicker
chocolate layer.
Pour over the wafers and put vanilla ice
cream on top. *Tip: use the rectangle box of
ice cream because it's easier to cut into
slices and lay out.
Make the ice cream layer about 1-inch thick.
Sprinkle the remaining wafers over the top.
Place in the freezer.

Cynthia's Pralines
Makes about 2 dozen

¾ c. buttermilk
2 c. sugar
2 c. pecan halves
1/8 tsp. salt
2 tbsp. butter
1 tsp. baking soda

Stir together buttermilk, sugar,
pecans, salt and butter in a 4 or
5-quart dish. Cook in the
microwave on high for 11
minutes. Stop and stir at 4
minute intervals.
Stir in the baking soda until
foamy. Cook on high for 1
minute. This gives the caramel
color.
Beat until tacky (about 1
minute). Drop by teaspoons on
foil and let cool.

Butterscotch Squares
Makes 9 squares (For when you need a simple indulgence!)

1 c. semi-sweet chocolate chips

1 - 14 oz. can sweetened condensed milk

1 c. chopped nuts

1 c. butterscotch chips

1 tsp. vanilla

Put chips and milk in top of a double boiler and stir until melted. Add nuts.
Pour mixture into buttered 9x7 glass baking dish.
Chill one hour. Cut into squares.

Ernesto's Grilled Salsa

Roast over a grill, 6 Anaheim green chilies, 5 yellow bell peppers and 6 medium tomatoes. Peel the chilies. Chop the peeled chilies, the tomatoes and the yellow peppers.

Finely dice 4 fresh jalapeños, 2 bundles of little green onions, and 1 bunch of cilantro (leaves only).

Mix all ingredients together and add 1 tsp. of vinegar. Salt to taste.

Vinegar helps to neutralize the heat in the chilies if you are not craving chili heat!

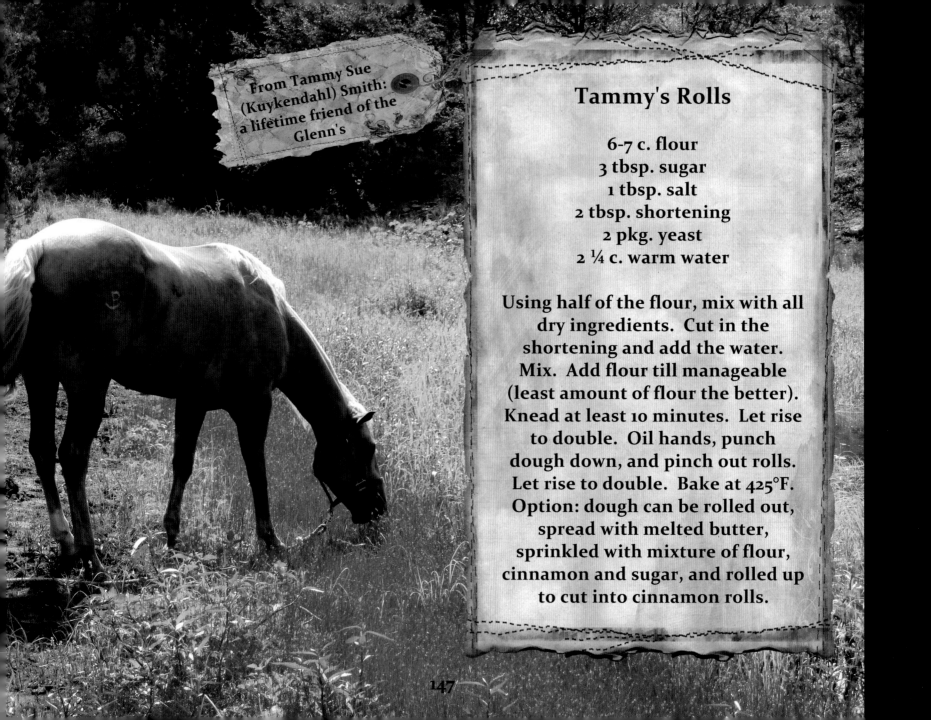

From Tammy Sue (Kuykendahl) Smith: a lifetime friend of the Glenn's

Tammy's Rolls

6-7 c. flour
3 tbsp. sugar
1 tbsp. salt
2 tbsp. shortening
2 pkg. yeast
2 ¼ c. warm water

Using half of the flour, mix with all dry ingredients. Cut in the shortening and add the water. Mix. Add flour till manageable (least amount of flour the better). Knead at least 10 minutes. Let rise to double. Oil hands, punch dough down, and pinch out rolls. Let rise to double. Bake at 425°F. Option: dough can be rolled out, spread with melted butter, sprinkled with mixture of flour, cinnamon and sugar, and rolled up to cut into cinnamon rolls.

Terry's Salsa

12 medium to large tomatoes, blanched
to remove the skins
1 large onion, chopped
3 bell peppers, chopped
6 hot peppers, preferably jalapeños,
chopped
¾ c. vinegar
3 tbsp. garlic salt
2 small 6-oz. cans tomato paste

Combine all ingredients and simmer
over medium-low heat for 2 to 3 hours,
stirring occasionally. If desired, you
may add some cornstarch to thicken.

Terry Feekes is a long-time family friend of
the Glenn's.
An Iowa farmer, he started coming out as a
lion hunting client 35 years ago, eventually
hunting Coues Deer, Mule Deer and Javelina
with our family.
Now Terry spends two weeks in late winter
with our family doing hard labor!
Great guy and a great friend.

The Todd's Ice Cream

For a large ice cream maker:
Makes 1 gallon

1 qt. milk
1 qt. cream
2 ½ c. sugar
2 tbsp. vanilla extract
½ tsp. salt

For small ice cream maker:
Makes 1/2 gallon

2 c. milk
2 c. cream
1 ¼ c. sugar
1 tbsp. vanilla extract
¼ tsp. salt

Combine ingredients, place in mixer. Follow mixer directions and allow to mix until frozen and ready to eat.

In the late 70's, early 80's, the Todd and Peterson families sold their ranches in Montana and moved to Arizona. They bought several ranches and became good friends and neighbors of the Glenn's. Through the years, the families worked a lot of cattle together, branding and joining efforts to catch some pretty wild cattle at times. Tom Todd also spent several years guiding deer and lion hunts with Marvin, Warner and Mom.
There were a lot of good meals shared and one of Mom's favorite recipes was JoAnn and Larry Todd's ice cream.

Two Tortillas

1

4 c. of flour
1 c. Crisco shortening
1 tbsp. salt
Room temperature/luke-warm water

Mix everything together by hand. Knead, adding water, until damp and mushy. Continue kneading till elastic. Put Crisco on your fingertips. Pat and mold dough into a large ball, then let rest 10 minutes. Make small balls and cover with a towel. Let them sit several hours.

Using a tortilla press, press out each dough ball, transfer to your hand and stretch tortilla into larger round shape.

Cook on a large hot griddle.

2

12 c. white flour
1 c. Crisco
1 heaping tbsp. salt
About 4 c. warm water

Put 10 - 10 ½ c. flour, Crisco, and salt in bowl and mix thoroughly by hand till even. Add the water a bit at a time, mixing constantly by hand in the bowl. Keep mixing and adding water until dough cleans side of bowl and is stiff. Turn from bowl onto unfloured surface and knead vigorously, stretching and mashing the dough until it's totally smooth and doesn't tear. Make into balls about 2-inches across by squeezing through your fist. Rub Crisco on your own hands and grease each ball. Place dough balls in bowl, cover and let rest 10 minutes. Heat griddle on high. Dip each ball lightly in flour. Roll out with a rolling pin, flipping and turning to keep shape round. Take into palm and stretch edges to final shape and size. Flip onto griddle. Cook about 10 seconds, flip and cover about 5-8 seconds, flip once more and cook about 5 seconds. Cool on a towel. When cool, stack less-done side up, put in plastic, and freeze.

Caldo de Queso

1 tsp. olive oil
3 roasted green chilies cut into strips or a small can
whole green chilies cut into strips
4 raw potatoes, peeled and cut into chunks
1 small raw onion, diced
1 small can tomato sauce
1 large fresh tomato, diced
1 c. chicken broth
Water, enough to cover the ingredients and bring to a
boil
A little salt
Queso fresco - whole milk cheese or Monterey Jack
cheese cut into chunks

Boil everything together until the potatoes are tender.
After potatoes are cooked, add cheese into soup and
serve as it is melting.
Optional: serve with a squeeze of lime juice!

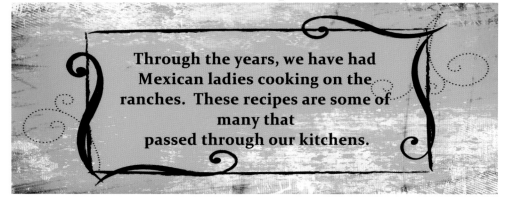

Through the years, we have had
Mexican ladies cooking on the
ranches. These recipes are some of
many that
passed through our kitchens.

Tamales

Wash and soften 12 corn husks. Cover with a damp cloth.
Food process 1 c. corn kernels with milk and a little water
until liquified.
Combine:
¼ c. butter
¼ c. Crisco shortening
¾ tsp. salt
1 tsp. sugar
1 tsp. baking powder
1 c. premixed masa harina
Liquid corn mixture from above
Mix well to consistency that is thick, soft and spreadable.
Add in ½ c. finely chopped green chili and 1 c. crumbled
queso fresco.
Add enough milk to make a workable consistency.
Spread a thin layer of dough on a husk. Add stick or
grated cheddar or Monterey Jack cheese onto the dough.
Roll the filled husk until closed, folding up the bottom
end.
Stand the tamales side by side and steam until firm about
40 minutes.

Arroz con Leche
(Rice Pudding)

1 c. rice
1 cinnamon stick
1 - 14 oz. can sweetened condensed milk
1 - 12 oz. can evaporated milk
Sugar
Boil rice as directed in water with cinnamon stick.
Add the sweetened condensed milk and evaporated
milk: mix and taste.
Add sugar to taste. Sprinkle cinnamon on top.

Beryl's Banana Split Dessert

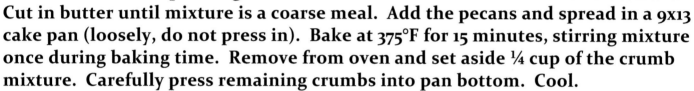

For the Vanilla Nut Crust
1 c. flour
1 - 4 oz. pkg. vanilla instant pudding mix
½ c. butter
½ c. finely chopped pecans

Combine flour and pudding mix.
Cut in butter until mixture is a coarse meal. Add the pecans and spread in a 9x13 cake pan (loosely, do not press in). Bake at 375°F for 15 minutes, stirring mixture once during baking time. Remove from oven and set aside ¼ cup of the crumb mixture. Carefully press remaining crumbs into pan bottom. Cool.

Layer #1:
2 bananas   2 tbsp. lemon juice
Slice the bananas ¼ inch thick and lightly dip in the lemon juice. Once the crust is cool, spread the sliced bananas over the mixture.

For the Filling:
¼ c. butter, softened   1 - 8 oz. pkg. cream cheese, softened
½ c. powdered sugar   1 - 8 oz. can crushed pineapple, drained
1 c. mini marshmallows
Combine butter, cream cheese, and powdered sugar. Beat until smooth and creamy. Stir in pineapple and mini marshmallows. Spread over the banana layer and refrigerate for 30 minutes.

J Bar A Ranch
2014
Brown Bear

My grandpa, Warner, was packing salt
with a pack horse and saw this bear
digging the middle out of a dead Mescal.
Warner stepped off his horse, dropped
the reins, sat down, rested his elbows on
his knees and proceeded to photograph
the local wildlife!

Mr. and Mrs. Ken Johnson are long-time supporters of the Arizona FFA. Ken was a long-time FFA Advisor and in retirement he continues to serve the FFA. It has been our pleasure to meet and know them and have several inspiring conversations. One such conversation initiated the contribution of two recipes to my book. The name of Mrs. Johnson's recipe is a conflicting mystery, however, a great recipe. Mr. Johnson's recipe needs you to be in the right place at the right time...

Mrs. Johnson's Smashed Cat

1 ½ to 2 lbs. ground lean meat
1 slightly beaten egg
1 chopped onion
2 to 3 drops liquid smoke

1 cup minute rice
1 can cream of mushroom soup
Salt and pepper to taste

Mix meat, rice, egg, onion, salt and pepper. Make into small balls. Mix soup and ½ can water and liquid smoke and pour over meat balls. Simmer with low heat or in oven at 350°F until done.

Karianne Johnson
Peoria, AZ

Mr. Johnson's Elephant Stew

1 medium size elephant
1 ton pepper
200 bushels of potatoes
2 small rabbits (optional)
gravy

1 ton salt
500 bushels carrots
4000 sprigs of parsley
1000 gallons of brown

Cut elephant into bite size pieces (this will take about 2 months).
Cut vegetables into cubes (allow another 2 months).
Place meat in pans and cover with 1,000 gallons of brown gravy and simmer gently for 4 weeks.
Shovel in salt and pepper to taste.
When meat is tender, add vegetables. Simmer slowly another 4 weeks.
Garnish with parsley.

Will serve 3,800 people. If more are expected or if some show up uninvited, add the 2 rabbits. This is not recommended as very few people like hare in their stew.

Ken Johnson, Peoria FFA Alumni
Arizona FFA Foundation Board Member

My Mom's Kitchen Wall

Our kitchen wall wraps into the dining room and upon it hangs an uninterrupted flow of things that I never really looked at, things that I just thought were trivial and cool. I asked Mom one day...
"What is all of this stuff?"
Her stories started with a small water color of a mountain lion laying on a bluff, painted by Mom's great aunt, Frankie Painter. A black and white photo of a young Marvin Glenn, my great-grandfather, hugging one of his lion hounds; an old photo of my other grandpa, Alfred Paul, sitting with a shotgun and his bird dog on a slew in old Mexico. There is a sandstone coaster as a reminder of the years that Mom participated in the Reba/Ben Johnson Pro Celebrity Rodeos at the Lazy E Arena in Edmond, Oklahoma. A black and white photo of myself at 3 years with my Dad, my grandpa Warner, western photographer Jay Dusard and neighbors David and Richard Moore, standing with their horses on the Mesa at the Malpai Ranch. They had been shooting a commercial for a commemorative gold coin. There is a picture of Warner loading cattle in the pens at the Gray Ranch in NM, the year that we were drougthed out and were given the opportunity to pasture our cattle over there. There is an old spur found on a ranch north of Douglas that our family used to own.

159

A ceramic angel with wings, a cowboy hat and a long braid given to my Mom by a dear friend.   An acrylic tile that says "From the bottom of my heart, Thank You" given to Mom by the High School Science teacher that helped Mom start restructuring the Douglas High School Land Lab.

There is a string of seeds and a crude pine bark angel carving that Mom collected when she was a teen and had accompanied her young brother, Cody, and my grandparents on a backpacking trip to Tarahumara Indian country in the Barranca Del Cobre in Mexico. There is a string of Mexican ceramic carved birds and a leather thong with brass bells given to my Mom by Wendy. There are several shell casings, .243 and .270, that Mom saved after she was successful in getting ahead of bluff running lions in the big horn sheep country in southwest New Mexico, killing them on the run as they fled from the hounds with no intention of baying.

There is a great photo of my Grandma Wendy on a mare named Ruby at the J Bar A. And a hand painted ceramic cross. There is a sitting burro, made of resin, made to accompany the Marguerite Henry story "Brighty of the Grand Canyon"...little did I know that in the early 1960's, my grandparents and great-grandpa Marvin had captured alive two big tom lions and hauled them to Kanab Utah to be in the movie!

There is a little swatch of black horse mane hair stuck in an empty shell casing doubling as a vase...cut from a horse named "Wood" that my grandparents raised and gave to my Dad after he married Mom. It was a horse that Wendy put a lot of miles on checking first calf heifers.

There is a live round, a .250 savage bullet, standing straight in the corner of a little cubby hole shelf. Mom found it on the floor of the J Bar A Bunkhouse, after drug runners had weathered out a storm there.

There is a cluster of dried roots that Mom hung to dry like wild flowers, a sculpture in its own...

160

Appropriately hanging among the root mass are two little wooden Cowbelle pins that belonged to one of my great-grandmothers and one of my great-great grandmothers! Another story from the past: when the original Cowbelles were formed in Douglas, AZ., the first social events were hosted in my great-great grandparents Ira and Marie Glenn's home. My great-great aunt Elsie Glenn suggested that a social organization be formed and with a unanimous vote and Mattie Cowan elected as the first President, the Cowbelles were founded.
Through the years, both sides of the family were involved: besides the original Glenn women, great-grandmother Virginia Paul, great-great grandmother Alice Holland, great-grandmother Margaret Glenn and grandmother Wendy were all Cowbelles.
Moving on, there are several little bouquets of dried roses, a turquoise stone egg, a rattlesnake rattle and several Mata Ortiz pots scattered throughout the collection. There is a bouquet of feathers all gathered on the ranches.
There is a larger photo of my grandpa Warner in his chaps, his back propped against a lichen covered boulder in the mountains somewhere, eating lunch.
There is an antique breakdown "Running Iron" in a leather scabbard that belonged to my great-great grandfather Ira Glenn.
There are several ceramic and wood carved ducks, birds and little Mexican pigs gracing the assorted shelf corners. There are old bottles, purple, brown and blue, stemming from my grandmother's extensive collection at the ranch. A Coues Deer antler hung as a chime with several metal crosses hanging from it, gracing our kitchen window.
Tucked into the collection is a note from my great grandmother "Tutu" to my Mom that says "Love You".
There are ornate, scrolled iron pieces, 2 lithographs of big hatted cowgirls and a deer antler completely covered with bling crystals, a gift to me from a friend in Santa Fe.

Hanging on the corner of a signed print of a vintage cowgirl is a string of turquoise beads, a gift to my Mom from a Mexican man from Chihuahua that worked for our family for 17 years.

There are a couple photos of me, both when I was about 3 years old, one with a calf-killing lion that we killed at the ranch. I had actually made the trek to where the dogs were barking treed! And in the other, I am wearing an old felt hat that had belonged to my great grandfather Marvin and the brim had been cut down to make it more applicable to a three year old.

There is a poster of the Indian Corn of the Americas and hanging on its corner is a string of black stone fetishes, Indian made. There are old west vintage ceramic tiles, steak-size branding irons, a quail cut out of metal, a shoulder mount of a Coues Deer buck Mom shot in New Mexico and an ornate metal chicken. A polished cow horn and an old dynamite box from the days that my grandmother's family owned a limestone quarry.

On the wall by the dining table there is a large 3x5 foot gold antique framed mirror that my great grandparents brought from Portugal. Next to it is a canvas original painting of an old adobe lodge that Mom and I bought on the Arizona Hopi Reservation. There is a metal photo of Warner, my friends Grant and Diego, myself and Wendy in the Steel Woods branding corral.

There is a shelf that Mom built using old wooden camp boxes from the days that my great grandpa Marvin and my grandpa Warner used to guide all their hunts from camp locations in old Mexico and Arizona. The ends are two old, narrow, Mexican mission-style doors and the top is a piece of tin from an old cotton wagon. The shelves hold lots of antlers, Mata Ortiz pots, lion skulls, old spurs, a large bull skull, an old purple glass kerosene lantern base, and a small selection of old western books, including Faye E. Ward's book The Cowboy at Work.

There is a handmade bit from the J Bar A, a pair of stainless spurs with a Jaguar etched in the side, commemorative of the first Jaguar that Warner photographed, and a small lithograph of a brahma steer. A large old glass jug holds ears of Indian corn and sycamore leaves collected on a hunt, a bible that Mom covered in leather, my graduating senior bouquet that Mom made me out of burlap roses and bling, and Jay Dusard's book, "The North American Cowboy, A Portrait," which has both a portrait of Wendy and Warner and also one of Marvin and Margaret in it.

Over our stove is a painting of a string of saddled horses tied to an old corral fence, next to the pantry is a photo of Mom's first Braford cow, an FFA project, the metal cutout words "Ranch", "Ride", "Rope", a vintage metal sign that was a Colt Firearms advertisement of a woman in a riding skirt with a Jaguar roped! Next to it is a close up photograph that my grandpa Warner took of a Jaguar that his hounds bayed in 1996. There are a series of large fish hooks from my grandmother's parents, used as they fished many of the bays in Old Mexico.

There is a little wooden box that mom turned into a shelf with peach seeds that Warner carved into boats and baskets when he was a young boy, two tiny vials of blond hair that Mom saved from the first time that I cut my own hair (they were my bangs until I cut them right off at the roots...made Mom cry!)

There is a series of little hand painted turtles, a metal cutout that says "FFA MOM", (and Mom was a good one), and a guitar pick used by my great grandfather.

I stood sobered and teary-eyed, so appreciative of the history that graced our kitchen walls in the form of an eclectic collection of mementos that Mom had placed with love and gratitude of her heritage. Every time I look at these walls now, I see things differently, and appreciate each facet even more.

Grateful cows and calves! Drought, unfortunately, always stands the test of time.

Chapter 7
Beef is Worth the Buck!

Individual Beef Wellingtons
Makes 10 servings - Prep time: 1 hour

1 lb. medium mushrooms	¼ c. butter	Salt
1 medium onion, minced	3 c. breadcrumbs	Water
½ tsp. pepper	¼ tsp. thyme leaves	
1 - 4 lb. beef rib eye roast	2 eggs, separated	

<u>Pastry Crust</u>: Wendy's Pie Crust (pg. 29). Make one recipe per Wellington.
Roll each crust out in 6" x 12" rectangles. Cut in half.
Remove stems from ten of the mushrooms, set mushroom caps aside. Mince
remaining mushrooms and extra stems.
In a large skillet, melt the butter over medium heat, add the minced mushrooms
and onion and cook for 5 minutes until all the liquid is evaporated. Stir in the
breadcrumbs, pepper, thyme, and 1 tsp. salt. Remove from heat and cool.
Trim fat off the roast and cut the meat in half lengthwise. Slice each half
crosswise into 5 equal pieces. Set aside.
Place 1/3 c. mushroom mixture in the center of one pastry rectangle. Top with a
piece of meat. Sprinkle meat lightly with salt. Top with 1 whole mushroom cap.
Beat egg whites with 2 tsp. water. Brush mixture over pastry edges. Fold pastry
over meat and mushroom, overlapping the edges; press to seal. Place the pocket
on a baking sheet. Repeat the assembly process for the remainder of the
pockets. About 35 minutes before serving, preheat the oven to 400°F. In a small
bowl, beat the egg yolks with 2 tsp. water; brush over pastry. Bake 25 minutes for
rare meat, 27 minutes for medium. Remove from oven and serve immediately.

Baked Boneless Chuck Steak with Breadcrumb Gravy

Servings: The volume of steak that you prepare will depend on the
number of people that you are planning to serve.
The following recipe serves 4

Preheat oven to 275°F.
Dissolve 1 cube of chipotle seasoning in 1 ½ c. red wine. Pour into the bottom
of a 9x13 glass baking dish.

Lightly salt and pepper both sides of 2 large boneless chuck steaks, with larger
chunks of fat trimmed off. Place steaks in baking dish with chipotle wine
liquid.   Top with 1 c. crushed
tomatoes. Spread over meat.

Spread 2 c. Italian
breadcrumbs over meat and
tomatoes.

Cover with foil and bake
at 275° F for 1 ½ - 2 hours.

Serve meat over rice with
breadcrumb gravy from
baking dish.

Malpai Ranch

167

No Sweat Round Steak
Serves 6 to 8 people

5 lb. round steak or cubed steak, trim off fat
1 - 14.5 oz. can Italian seasoned diced tomatoes
1 c. red wine
1 - 14.5 oz. can beef broth
2 c. Italian breadcrumbs

Preheat oven to 350°F.
Combine the wine, broth and tomatoes in a medium bowl. Pour 1/3 of the liquid into the bottom of a 9x13 casserole dish. Lay the meat into the bottom of the baking dish, leaving no gaps. Pour the remaining liquid over the top. Liberally sprinkle the breadcrumbs over the meat, covering the meat completely. Cover with aluminum foil and bake to desired doneness. Uncover and bake 10 more minutes to make the top nice and crispy.

If you unexpectedly find out that you'll be hosting company tonight, and it's already the middle of the afternoon, this hearty dish fits the bill for its easy prep, quick cook, and bold flavors.

Hawaiian Beef Stew
Serves 4-6

Beef for this recipe can be cut from a number of different roasts, arm and chuck steaks, etc.

2 lbs. beef stew meat, cut into chunks
1 ½ c. canned or fresh pineapple chunks, drained
1 c. pineapple juice
1 c. green bell pepper, diced
¼ c. onion, diced
½ c. papaya nectar
¼ c. Tequila
2 tbsp. ketchup
Water to ensure there is enough liquid to cover all ingredients.
Place all ingredients in a slow cooker. Turn on to low setting if you are going to be out all day, and high if you want to eat this meal in 4-6 hours.

*The meat will definitely take on the pineapple flavor.

Italian Roasted Prime Rib
Serves 10 - 12

1 tbsp. chopped fresh thyme
1 tbsp. chopped fresh rosemary
1 tbsp. kosher salt
1 tsp. freshly ground black pepper
3 cloves garlic, minced
1 c. sweet red wine
1 c. low-sodium beef broth
1 - 14.5 oz. can Italian seasoned diced tomatoes
1 - 6 lb. beef prime rib roast, trussed

Preheat the oven to 425°F. Place an oven rack in the center of the oven.

Allow the beef to stand for 30 minutes at room temperature before roasting.

Mix together the thyme, rosemary, salt, pepper, garlic, wine, broth, and tomatoes in a medium bowl. Make 1-inch long, ½-inch deep slits all over the meat using a paring knife. Rub the garlic mixture into the slits and onto the rest of the meat. Place the meat, fat-side up, in a shallow roasting pan. Roast for 45 minutes. Cover the meat with foil and continue to roast until a meat thermometer inserted straight down into the center of the meat registers 145°F for medium-rare, 65 to 75 minutes. Place the roast on a baking sheet and tent with foil. Allow to rest for 20 minutes before slicing.

Sauce

2 c. low-sodium beef broth
1 c. sweet red wine
1 tbsp. chopped fresh thyme
1 tsp. minced fresh white onion
3 tbsp. unsalted butter, at room temperature, cut into
1/2-inch cubes
1 ½ tsp. kosher salt
½ tsp. freshly ground black pepper

Combine any juices from the rested meat with the broth,
wine, thyme, and onion in a medium saucepan.
Bring to a boil, stirring constantly. Reduce the heat and
simmer until thick, 20 minutes.

Whisk in the butter until smooth and season with salt and
pepper. Pour the sauce into a serving dish with a ladle.

Slice the roast into ½-inch-thick slices and serve with sauce.

Herbed Prime Rib & Sauces
Serves 12

1 - 5 lb. beef rib roast
1 c. beef broth
1/2 c. Merlot wine
1 tbsp. dry mustard
1 1/2 tsp. instant coffee powder
1 tsp. garlic salt
1 tsp. onion powder
1/2 tsp. dried thyme, crushed
1/2 tsp. dried oregano, crushed
1/2 tsp. ground coriander
1/2 tsp. celery seeds
1 tbsp. olive oil

Preheat oven to 350° F.
Make dry rub: in small bowl, combine mustard, coffee powder, garlic salt, onion powder, thyme, oregano, coriander and celery seeds. Set aside.
Rub olive oil over roast. Sprinkle with dry rub. Cut slices in the fat and rub in the dry rub using your fingers.
Place roast fat-side-up in a large roasting pan. Insert an oven-going thermometer into the center of the roast. Roast for 1 3/4 to 2 3/4 hours until thermometer reads 135°F for medium rare or 150°F for medium.
Transfer roast to cutting board. Cover with foil. Let stand 15 minutes before carving.
Serve with the following sauces.

Merlot Au Jus
Makes 1 c.

Roast drippings
1 1/2 c. beef broth
1/2 c. Merlot Wine
2 tsp. Worcestershire sauce
1 tbsp. water
1-2 tsp. cornstarch

Remove roast from roasting pan. Pour drippings into large glass measuring cup. Skim off fat and discard.
Add broth, Merlot and Worcestershire sauce drippings. Pour back into pan. Heat and stir over medium heat until bubbly, scraping up crusty browned bits from bottom of pan.
For a thicker au jus, stir together the water and cornstarch. Whisk into bubbling broth mixture.

If desired, strain au jus before serving.

Dipping Cream
Makes 1 3/4 c.

1 - 8 oz. container sour cream
1/2 c. mayonnaise
2 tsp. Dijon-style mustard
2 tsp. white wine vinegar

Optional: 2 tsp. prepared horseradish

In small bowl, combine sour cream, mayonnaise, mustard and white wine vinegar.

Cover and chill.
Serve with the Prime Rib.

174

Hearty Beef and Tortilla Strip Soup

Serves 10

3 celery stalks, diced

1 quart water

3 green chiles, diced

1 - 10 oz. bag grated carrots

1 stick (1/2 c.) butter

Weber Steak 'n Chop seasoning

½ c. tequila

1 - 32 oz. carton beef broth

1 - 14.5 oz. can Italian Seasoned diced tomatoes

8 medium potatoes, peeled and cubed

3 large chunks roasted red bell peppers, diced

2 lb. beef stew meat, cut into smaller chunks

1 large white onion, sliced into rings

Chipotle Cheddar Tortilla Strips, for garnish

In a large soup pot, combine celery, beef broth, water, tomatoes, potatoes, green chilies, and bell peppers.

In a large skillet, sear the beef strips on all sides and season with hearty sprinkling of Steak 'n Chop seasoning. Add meat strips and grated carrots to soup pot.

In the same skillet the beef was cooked in, melt the butter. Slowly add in the tequila. Add the raw onion rings. Cook over medium heat until tender and almost translucent.

Add the tequila onions and cooking liquid into the soup pot and simmer over medium heat for one hour.

Top with grated fiesta cheese blend and Chipotle Cheddar Tortilla Strips

175

Douglas Dispatch

October 2, 1940

Christainsen Cattle Sold to Glenn to Ship
to Coast. Three carloads of cows and calves
were purchased yesterday by Ira D. Glenn
from H. L. Christainsen to be loaded next Monday
for shipment to Strathearn, Calif., not far from Fresno.
The price paid for the shipment was announced as nine
cents straight across, for the calves and four and five
cents for the cows.

My great-great-grandpa was Ira Glenn

Mesquite Beef Brisket

Serves 6-8
Preheat oven to 300°F.

1 medium beef brisket
1 tbsp. mesquite spice rub
Mix together:
1 cube onion seasoning,
    dissolved in 1 cup water
½ c. Pendleton whiskey
½ c. liquid mesquite marinade

Lightly rub brisket with mesquite rub.
Place brisket in glass baking dish.
Pour liquid mixture over brisket. If more liquid is desired, add a little more water. Cover with foil. Bake until desired preference.

Glenn Cattle, Fall Shipping, Diamond A Ranch, SW New Mexico

Tangy Beef Brisket

Serves 6 - 8

1 medium beef brisket
1 small jar Worcestershire sauce
1 small jar soy sauce
1 tsp. ground ginger
½ cup orange juice

Combine Worcestershire sauce, soy sauce, ginger and orange juice.
Place brisket in glass baking dish. Cover with liquid mixture. Cover with foil. Marinate 2- 4 hours.
Preheat oven to 300°F.
Cook brisket to your preference.
Slice and serve.

My Mom (Kelly) attended college at San Luis Obispo, California and worked for JoAnn Switzer on the Madonna and Twisselman ranches. It was a great time in her life, she made lots of good friends, was always provided with good horses to ride and participated in huge branding's which always ended in incredible barbecues.

Tri-tips were usually the meat of choice, so Mom created the following recipe to marinate them with and has served up to 500 people off the grill.

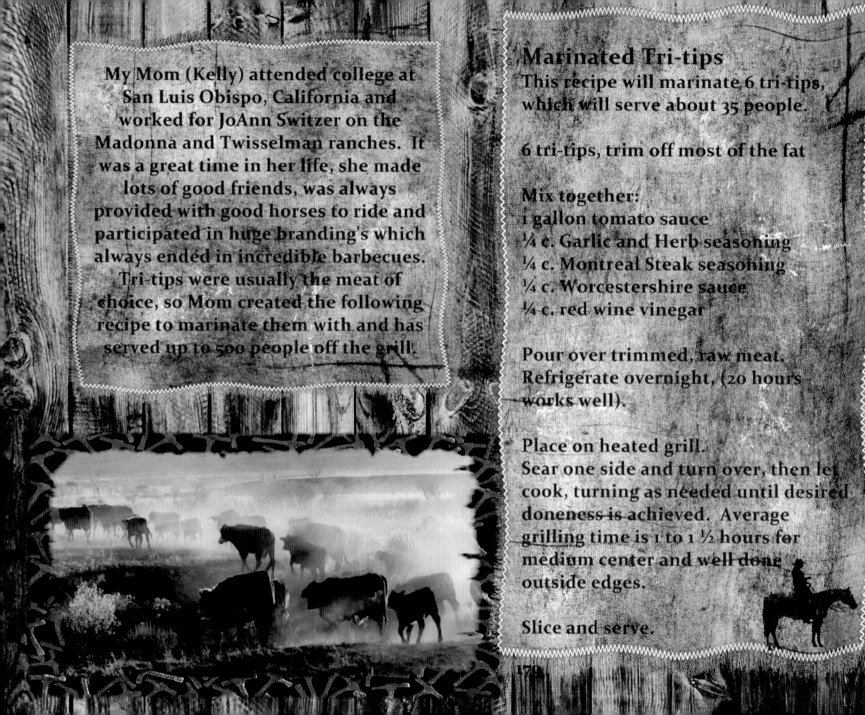

Marinated Tri-tips

This recipe will marinate 6 tri-tips, which will serve about 35 people.

6 tri-tips, trim off most of the fat

Mix together:
1 gallon tomato sauce
¼ c. Garlic and Herb seasoning
¼ c. Montreal Steak seasoning
¼ c. Worcestershire sauce
¼ c. red wine vinegar

Pour over trimmed, raw meat. Refrigerate overnight, (20 hours works well).

Place on heated grill.
Sear one side and turn over, then let cook, turning as needed until desired doneness is achieved. Average grilling time is 1 to 1 ½ hours for medium center and well done outside edges.

Slice and serve.

Eye of the Round

Variations from a commonly available, inexpensive cut of beef.
These recipes can be easily altered based on how many people you are serving.

1 Roast beef sandwich meat

Roast the whole eye of the round in one or two packages of Lipton onion soup mix, mixed in water as directed on the package, at 350°F until desired doneness is reached. Remove from oven and let rest until room temperature. Slice very thinly across the grain. Makes great roast beef sandwich meat!

2 Papaya Beef
Preheat oven to 275°F.

1 average-sized raw Eye of the Round roast, sliced thinly with the grain of the meat
1 small to medium-sized papaya, sliced in rounds ½" thick

Mix together in a separate bowl and set aside:
½ c. Catalina salad dressing
4 tbsp. pineapple juice
4 tbsp. papaya nectar (can be purchased in the fruit juice isle)

Most inexpensive cuts of beef can be cooked and tenderized with recipe 2, 3, 4 & 5.

Arrange sliced papaya in the bottom of a glass baking dish.
Lightly salt and pepper both sides of each slice of meat. Layer meat on papaya.
Pour dressing mix over beef and papaya.
Cover with foil and bake 1 ½ - 2 hours until desired doneness is reached.

3 Green Chili Beef Wrap

Preheat oven to 275°F.

1 Eye of the round beef roast, thinly sliced with the grain into steaks
1 large can whole green chili
1 small can green chili enchilada sauce

Roll one whole green chili into each steak.
Place rolled steaks side by side in bottom of glass baking dish. Cover meat with green chili enchilada sauce.
Cover with foil and bake for 1 ½ to 2 hours.

4 Pendleton Whiskey Green Chile Beef Wrap

Preheat oven to 275°F.

1 Eye of the round beef roast, thinly sliced with the grain into steaks
1 can whole green chili
Salt and pepper steaks very lightly
Mix together, (for 9 x 11 glass baking dish):
1 c. Pendleton Whiskey
1 tsp. garlic powder
Roll one green chili in each steak, then place side by side in baking dish.
Pour whiskey mixture over meat.
Cover with foil and bake 1 ½ hours or until desired doneness is reached.

5 Tequila Green Chile Beef Wrap

Same recipe as above, but substitute Pendleton Whiskey with Tequila and 1 tsp. lime juice.

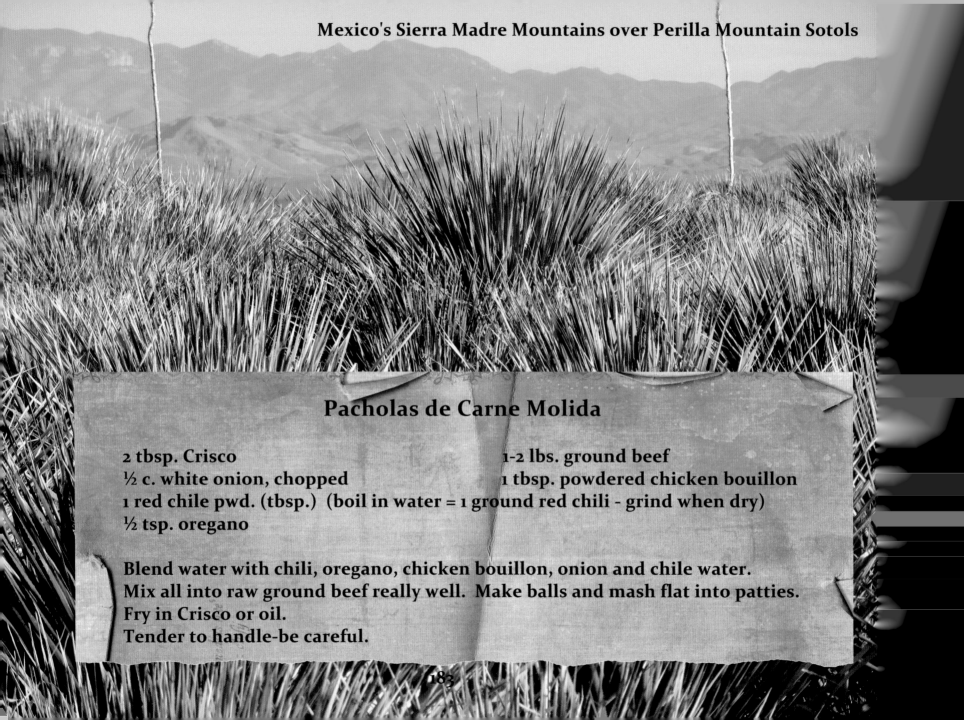

Pacholas de Carne Molida

2 tbsp. Crisco   1-2 lbs. ground beef
½ c. white onion, chopped   1 tbsp. powdered chicken bouillon
1 red chile pwd. (tbsp.) (boil in water = 1 ground red chili - grind when dry)
½ tsp. oregano

Blend water with chili, oregano, chicken bouillon, onion and chile water.
Mix all into raw ground beef really well. Make balls and mash flat into patties.
Fry in Crisco or oil.
Tender to handle-be careful.

Sonoran Beef Stew
Serves 4-6

2 lbs. beef stew meat
1 - 30 oz. can hominy, drained
1 c. green enchilada sauce
1-2 tomatillos, diced (canned tomatillos add a saltier flavor to the dish)
¼ c. tequila
½ c. mild salsa
Juice from 2 medium limes

Place all ingredients in slow cooker. Add enough water to insure all ingredients are covered. Turn on to low setting if you are going to be out all day, and high if you want to eat this meal in 4-6 hours.

If a spicier stew is desired, substitute the mild salsa for hot and add a diced hot chili like jalapeño or habanero.

Beef for this recipe can be cut from a number of different roasts, arm and chuck steaks, etc.

Beef Short Ribs with Pendleton Whiskey

Preheat oven to 275°F.

6 beef short ribs
½ c. Pendleton whiskey
1 - 28 oz. can crushed tomatoes
½ c. diced onions
½ c. pineapple juice
1 small apple, chopped
Juice of 2 medium limes

Place ribs in baking dish.

Mix together whiskey, tomatoes, onions, pineapple juice, apple and lime juice.

Pour mixture over ribs.

Cover and bake until meat reaches desired doneness.

Tequila Beef Short Ribs

Preheat oven to 275°F.

4 beef short ribs
Seasoned meat tenderizer
½ c. tequila
Juice of 2 medium limes
1 tomatillo, diced
½ c. green enchilada sauce

Sprinkle short ribs with meat tenderizer.
Place in glass baking dish.

Mix tequila, lime juice, tomatillo and enchilada sauce.
Pour over ribs.

Bake until meat has reached desired doneness.

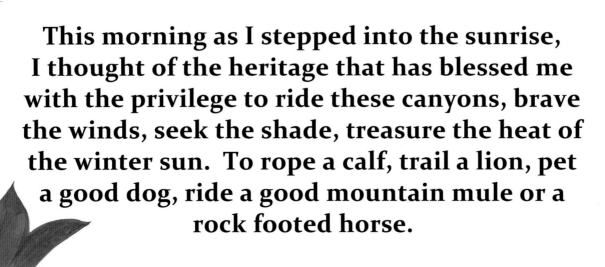

This morning as I stepped into the sunrise, I thought of the heritage that has blessed me with the privilege to ride these canyons, brave the winds, seek the shade, treasure the heat of the winter sun. To rope a calf, trail a lion, pet a good dog, ride a good mountain mule or a rock footed horse.

Time ticks by, the small things are forgotten or taken for granted, every moment is lost in time and we seem to forget to treasure instead of judge. We are so blessed to have God, Family, Country and Freedom.

Thank you to my relatives past, my grandparents and parents present and the opportunities in the future. This life and my time here is truly a blessing, and I am grateful.

J-A

MALPAI RANCH
Purchased
1960

J BAR A RANCH
Homesteaded
1896-1907

-O-

Acknowledgements

In the development of this book, the following digital content was used:

Berks Lane Kit, Catana, Coastal, Sun Porch: copyright Katie Pertiet, Designer Digitals. com, Click Creative Group. Inc.

Base Coat I, II, III: copyright Kaisercraft (Panstoria.com, Artisan.com)

Art Journal Clipboards No.3, Beloved Page Pak, Everyday Paper Pak No.6, Get it Framed 2 Dangles, Nature's Sketchbook Papers 2 Harmony, Painter's Canvas Paper Pak No.1, Spring Medley Element Pak, Winged Beauty: copyright Cottage Arts.net LLC.

Bright Kit, Earth Sampler, Vintage Memories Frames & Mats, Vintage memories Kit: copyright Panstoria, Inc. Personal

Boots & Braids Digital Kit, Boots & Buckles Digital Kit, Brush Strokes, Dress it Up Digital Embellishments, Elements Digital Embellishments, Frames & Borders, Reminisce Autumn, Reminisce Spring, Nature Digital Embellishments, Painted Swirls, Puffy Vines, Vintage Romance Sewing Room Digital Embellishments, Reminisce Digital Power Palette, Autumn Breeze, Black & White Digital, Cheerful Christmas Digital Additions, Cheerful Winter Digital Additions, Hunting Digital Additions, Untamed, Earthy Serenity Digital Additions, Modern Kitchen, Primary Christmas, Recipe Book Digital Kit, Savannah Digital Kit: Creative Memories

All above kits available through Panstoria Artisan 4.

Photography
Warner Glenn, Kelly Glenn-Kimbro, Raymond Harris, Mackenzie Kimbro.

Old photography courtesy of Glenn and Paul family albums and archives.

Special Thanks:
To my mom, Kelly,
for the drive and determination to help me pull this book together, for giving me encouragement, for helping me through this past summer of tough times as we dealt with the raw emotions of losing Wendy, and then for helping me try to pay tribute to her through this book. You mean the world to me, I love you.

To my grandpa, Warner,
for tolerating the long hours we spent away from ranch duties in the process of writing this book, for teaching me the ways of ranching and cattle, and for supporting me in whatever endeavours I have taken on over the years. You are my hero, and I love you.

To my dad, Kerry,
for being a part of our support crew, and for cooking some mean dinners for us when we least expected them! Love you Dad!

And to all of the folks that were a part of the village that raised me, thank you for everything. I am forever grateful to all of you for showing me great friendships, grand adventures, good food and lots of fun.
Here's to good rains and fat cattle!

Nothing brings people together like good food...

Be Creative!